An Introduction to Business Analytics

An Introduction to Business Analytics

Ger Koole

MG books
Amsterdam

Preface

Books on Business Analytics (BA) typically fall into two categories: managerial books without any technical details, and very technical books, written for BA majors who already have a background in advanced mathematics or computer science. This book tries to fill the gap by discussing BA techniques at a level appropriate for readers with a less technical background. This makes it suitable for many different audiences, especially managers who want to better understand the work of their data scientists, or people who want to learn the basics of BA and do their first BA projects themselves.

The full range of BA-related topics is covered: from the many different techniques to an overview of managerial aspects; from comparisons of the usefulness of different techniques in different situations to their historical context. While working with this book, you will also learn appropriate tooling, especially R and a bit of Excel. There are exercises to sharpen your skills and test your understanding.

Because this book contains a large variety of topics, I sought advice from many experts. I am especially indebted to Sandjai Bhulai, Bram Gorissen, Jeroen van Kasteren, Diederik Roijers and Qingchen Wang for their feedback on scientific issues and Peggy Curley for editing.

Business Analytics is a young field in full development, which uses aspects from various fields of science. Although I tried to integrate the knowledge from many fields, it is unavoidable that the content will be biased based on my background and experience. Please do not hesitate to send me an email if you have any ideas or comments to share. I sincerely hope that reading this book is a rewarding experience.

All chapters can be read independently, but I advise to read Chapter 1 first to understand the connections between the chapters. The index at the end can be helpful for unknown terms and abbreviations.

Ger Koole   Amsterdam/Peymeinade, 2016–2019

i

Contents

Chapter 1

Introduction

This chapter explains business analytics and data science without going into any technical detail. We will clarify the meaning of different terms used, put the current developments in a historical perspective, give the reader an idea of the potential of business analytics (BA), and give a high-level overview of the steps and pitfalls in implementing a BA strategy.

Learning outcomes   On completion of this chapter, you will be able to:

- describe in non-technical terms the field of business analytics, the different steps involved, the connections to other fields of study and its historical context

- reflect on the skills and knowledge required to successfully apply business analytics in practice

1.1   What is business analytics?

According to Wikipedia, "Business analytics refers to the skills, technologies, practices for continuous iterative exploration and investigation of past business performance to gain insight and drive business planning." In short, BA is a rational, fact-based approach to decision making. These facts come from data, therefore BA is about the science and the skills to turn data into decisions. The science is mostly *statistics*, *artificial intelligence* (*data mining* and *machine learning*), and *optimization*; the skills are computer skills, communication skills, project and change management, etc.

It should be clear that BA by itself is not a science. It is the total set of knowledge that is required to solve business problems in a rational way. To be a successful business analyst, experience in BA projects and knowledge of the business areas that the data comes from (such as healthcare, advertising, finance) is also very valuable.

BA is often subdivided into three consecutive activities: *descriptive analytics*, *predictive analytics*, and *prescriptive analytics*. During the descriptive phase, data is analyzed and patterns are found. The insights are consequently used in the predictive phase to predict what is likely to happen in the future, if the situation remains the same. Finally, in the prescriptive phase, alternative decisions are determined that change the situation and which will lead to desirable outcomes.

Example 1.1 *A hotel chain analyzes its reservations to look for patterns: which are the busiest days of the week? What is the impact of events in the city? Is there a seasonal pattern? Etc. The outcomes are used to make a prediction for the revenue in the upcoming months. By changing the pricing of the rooms in certain situations (such as sports events), the expected revenue can be maximized.*

Analytics can only start when there is data. Certain organizations already have a centralized *data warehouse* in which relevant current and historical data is stored for the purpose of reporting and analytics. Setting up such a data warehouse and maintaining it is part of the *business intelligence* (BI) strategy of a company. However, not all companies have such a centralized database, and even when it exists it rarely contains all the information required for a certain analysis. Therefore, data often needs to be collected, cleansed and combined with other sources. Data collection, cleansing and further pre-processing is usually a very time-consuming task, often taking more time than the actual analysis.

Example 1.2 *In the hotel revenue management example above we need historical data on reservations but also data on historical and future events in the surroundings of the hotel. There are many reasons why this data can be hard to get: reservation data may only be stored at an aggregated level, there may have been changes in IT systems which overrode previously collected data, there may be no centrally available list with events, etc. Many organizations assume they already have all the data required, but as soon as the data scientist asks for reservation data combined with the date the booking was made or the event list from the surrounding area, the hotel might find out that they lack data.*

Therefore, data collection and pre-processing are always the first steps of a BA project. Following the data collection and pre-processing the real data science steps begin with descriptive analytics. Moreover, a BA project does not end with prescriptive analytics, i.e., with generating an (optimal) decision. The decision has to be implemented, which requires various skills, such as knowledge of change management.

To summarize, we distinguish the following steps in a BA project:

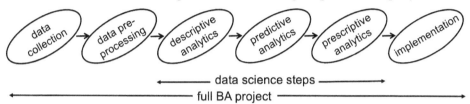

The model above suggests a linear process, but in practice this is rarely the case. At many of the steps, depending on the outcome, you might revisit earlier steps. For example, if the predictions are not accurate enough for a particular aaplication then you might collect extra data to improve them. Furthermore, not all BA projects include prescriptive analytics, many projects have insight or prediction as goal and therefore finish after the descriptive or predictive steps.

The major scientific fields of study corresponding to these BA steps are:

Next to cleansing, *feature engineering* is an important part of data preparation, to be discussed later. During descriptive analytics you get an understanding of the data. You visualize the data and you summarize it using the tool of statistical data analysis. Getting a good understanding is crucial for making the right choices in the consecutive steps.

Following the descriptive analytics a BA project continues with predictive analytics. A target value is specified which we want to predict. Based on the data available, the parameters of the selected predictive method are determined. We say that the model is *trained* on the data. The methods originate from inferential statistics and machine learning, which have their respective roots in mathematics and computer science. Although the approach and the background of these fields are quite different, the techniques largely overlap.

Example 1.3 *A debt collection agency wants to use its resources, mainly calls to debtors, in a better way. It collects data on payments which is enriched by external data on household composition and neighborhood characteristics. After the data analysis and visualization a method is selected that predicts, given the characteristics of the dept and the actions taken by the agency, the probability that the deptor will pay off their debt. In the prescriptive step, which is to be discussed next, the best action for each deptor is determined.*

Finally, during the prescriptive analytics phase, options are found to maximize a certain objective. Because the future is always unpredictable to a certain extent, optimization techniques often have to account for this randomness. The field that specializes in this is (mathematical) *optimization*. It overlaps partially with *reinforcement learning*, which has its roots in computer science. A special feature of reinforcement learning is that prediction and optimization are integrated: it combines in one method the predictive and prescriptive phases.

Example 1.4 *Consider again Example 1.2 on hotel revenue management. After having studied the influence of events and for example intra-week fluctuations on hotel reservations in the descriptive step demand per price class is* forecasted *in the predictive step. These forecasts are input to an optimization algorithm that determines on a daily basis the prices that maximize total revenue.*

We end this section by discussing two terms that are closely related to BA: *Data science* and *big data*. Data science is an older term which has recently shifted in meaning and increased in popularity. It is a combination of different scientific fields all concerned with extracting knowledge from data, mainly data mining and statistics. Part of the popularity probably stems from the fact that the Harvard Business Review called a data scientist role "the sexiest job of 21st century", anticipating the huge demand for data scientists. The knowledge base of data scientists and business analysts largely overlap. However, the deliverable of BA is improved business performance, whereas data scientists focus more on methods and insights from data. Improved business performance requires optimization to generate decisions and *soft skills* to implement the decisions.

Finally, a few words on big data. Big data differentiates itself from regular data sets by the so-called 3 V's: *volume*, *variety*, and *velocity*. A data

> **Box 1.1. From randomized trials to using already available data**
> The traditional way to do scientific research in the medical and behavorial sciences is through (double-blind) *randomized trials*. This means that subjects (e.g., patients) have to be selected, and by a randomized procedure they are made part of the trial or part of the control group. It is called double blind when the subject and the researcher are both not aware of who is in which group. This kind of research set-up allows for a relatively simple statistical analysis, but it is often hard to implement and very time-consuming.
> Nowadays, data can often be obtained from Electronic Health Records and other data sources. This eliminates the need for separate trials. However, there will be all kinds of statistical *biases* in the data, making it harder to make a fair comparison between treatments. For example, patients of a certain age or having certain symptoms might get more-often a certain treatment. This calls for advanced statistical methods to eliminate these biases. These methods are usually not taught in medical curricula, requiring the help of expert data scientists.

set is considered to be "big data" when the amount of data is too much to be stored in a regular database, when it lacks a homogeneous structure (i.e., free text instead of well-described fields), and/or when it is only available real-time. Big data requires adapted storage systems and analysis techniques in order to exploit it.

Big data now receives a lot of attention due to the speed at which data is collected these days. As more and more devices and sensors automatically generating data are connected to the internet (the *internet of things*) again, the amount of stored data doubles approximately every 3 years. However, most BA projects do not involve big data, but use with relatively small and structured data sets. It might have been the case that such a dataset had its origin in big data from which relevant information has been extracted.

Example 1.5 *Cameras in metro stations are used to surveil passengers. Using image recognition software the numbers of passengers can be extracted, which can be used as input for a prediction method that forecasts future passenger volumes.*

1.2 Historical overview

Business analytics combines techniques from different fields all originating from their own academic background. We will touch upon the main constituent fields of statistics, artificial intelligence, *operations research*, and also BA and data science (DS).

Statistics is a mathematical discipline with a large body of knowledge developed in the pre-computer age. For many decades, statistics has been taught at universities without the use of any data sets. The central body of knowledge concerns the behavior of statistical quantities in limiting situations, for example when the number of observations approaches infinity. This is of a highly mathematical nature. More recently new branches of statistics have come into existence, many of which are more experimental in nature. However, quite often statistics is still taught as a mathematical discipline with a focus on the mathematics.

Artificial intelligence (AI) is a field within computer science that grew rapidly from the 1970s with the advent of computers.

Initial expectations were highly inflated. One believed, for example, that so-called *expert systems* would soon replace doctors in their work of diagnosing illnesses in patients. This did not happen and the attention for AI diminished. Today, the expectations are high again, largely due the fields of *data mining* and *machine learning* which are relevant for BA. They developed more recently when large data sets became available for analysis. Both fields of data mining and machine learning focus on learning from data and making predictions using what is learned. Machine learning focuses on predictive models, data mining more broadly on the process from data pre-processing to predictive analytics, with a focus on data-driven methods. The difference between statistics and machine learning are their origins and the more data-oriented approach of ML: Mathematicians want to prove theoretically that things work, computer scientists want to show it using data.

Operations research (OR) is about the application of mathematical optimization to decision problems in organizations. OR, sometimes called *management science*, and abbreviated as OR/MS, also raised big expectations, in the 1950s, following the first successes of the allied forces of OR being applied during World War II. The belief was that scientific methods would replace traditional management and turn it into a science. However, the impact at the strategic decision level remained very limited and OR applications are mainly found at the operational level. Quite often the application of OR would be to a logistical problem such as the routing of delivery vans, outside the scope of higher management. OR faces the same problems as statistics: it has been developed as a highly mathematical science, but it has a hard time adapting itself to the current situation in which data and tooling is easily available. Often it is still taught in a highly abstract mathematical way, limiting the potential impact in practice.

BA on the other hand, developed in organizations that realized that their data was not just valuable for their current operations, but also to gain insight and improve their processes. Starting in the 1990's, we saw more and more analysts working with data in organizations. An important difference with OR is that many executives do understand the value of analytics and adopt a company-wide BA strategy. A book by Davenport [8], who is an advocate of BA, also played a role in increasing the interest in the value of analytics to executives. Interestingly enough, the main example throughout the book is dynamic pricing in airlines, a typical OR success. The name OR is not mentioned once. This supports the opinion that some of these new areas are in fact rebranded old areas, it's old wine in a new bottle. Whether this is really true, or if there are fundamental differences between areas is not really relevant. The fact is that the availability of data, computers and software made the widespread use of BA possible. Finally, BA methods—also the ones originating from the mathematical sciences—are used on a huge scale in companies, institutions and research centers, offering countless opportunities for business analysts and data scientists.

DS as a term has been around for a long time. In the end of the last century it was mainly associated with statistics. Much like BA, the term became popular with the availability of large data sets. However, today it is moreoften associated with techniques from computer science such as machine learning. In contrast, BA is more often associated with mathematics and industrial engineering.

1.3 Non-technical overview

In this section we give a non-technical overview of the most often used techniques and explain some of the technical terms that are regularly used. This section by nature can only be an oversimplification of reality, but it will help to get a flavor of the totality of the field, which even professionals in the field sometimes do not have. The techniques we discuss in this section are summarized in Figure 1.1.

The four steps pre-processing, descriptive, predictive and prescriptive analytics, can also be described as follows:
- preparing the data set;
- understanding the data set;
- predicting a target value;
- maximizing the target value.

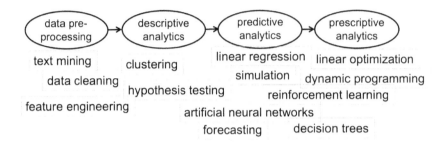

Figure 1.1: An overview of the most-often used data science techniques

Most predictive techniques require that you first structure the data. For example, topics can be extracted from text entered on social media or types of objects can be extracted from images. This brings us to a first distinction: between *structured* and *unstructured* data. Structured data usually consists of entries (e.g., people) with attributes (e.g., name, income, sex, nationality). The possible value for the attributes are well-defined (e.g., numerical, M/F, standard country codes). Structured data can be represented as a *matrix*: the rows are the entries, the columns the attributes.

Structured data comes in different flavors: for example, it can be numerical (e.g., temperature), categorical (e.g., days of the week), binary (e.g., true/false). Depending on the type of data different algorithms or adaptations of algorithms are used. If we have *univariate* data, i.e., data with only one attribute, then we can look at the distribution or compare different data sets. For *multivariate* data we can study how the different attributes influence each other.

Unstructured data has no such structure. It might be data from cameras, social-media sites, text entered in free text fields, etc. Counted in bytes, unstructured data is the majority of the data that is stored today, and it is often also big data. However, most of the BA and DS projects involve structured data, on which we will focus. When working with unstructured data, the first step is often to extract *features* to make it structured and therefore suitable as input for an algorithm working with structured data (e.g., images from road-side cameras are used to extract license plates which are then used to analyze the movement of cars).

Dealing with unstructured data is an important part of the pre-processing step. Cleansing is another one. Data often contains impossible values or empty fields. Different techniques exist to deal with these. A final important pre-processing activity is *feature engineering*, combining attributes or *features* into new potentially more useful attributes. For example, combining "day of week" and "time" can lead to an attribute "business hours", and postal codes of individuals combined with census data can lead to an approximation of income and family composition.

Next we explore the data in the descriptive step. Typical activities are visualisation, different statistical techniques such as *hypothesis testing*, and *clustering*. Visualization is a technique as old as humanity, but it has developed tremendously over the last decades. Exploratory statistics will be discussed in Chapter 3. In clustering, you look for data points that are in some mathematical sense close together. Think about clustering individuals based in income, sex, age and family composition for marketing purposes.

In the descriptive step we do not focus on a target value (such as sales or number of patients cured). Having a target value is the defining distinction of predictive analytics. Therefore predictive analytics is also called *supervised learning*: we learn an algorithm to predict a target value based on a data set with known target values. In contrast, techniques such as clustering are considered *unsupervised learning*.

Supervised learning comes in two flavors: *regression* and *classification*. In regression we estimate a numerical value. The best-known methods are *linear regression* and *artificial neural networks* (which is actually a form of non-linear regression), but other methods exist. In classification, the outcome is membership of two or more classes, e.g., whether or not somebody will click on an online ad, or vote on one of a number of parties. Most methods for regression can be adapted such that they can classify as well. Machine learning covers both supervised and unsupervised learning.

Box 1.2. Human versus artificial intelligence

Certain AI techniques are inspired by human intelligence or structures we find in nature, illustrated by names such as *artificial neural networks* or *evolutionary computing*. It is an interesting question whether or not we should try to copy human behavior with, eventually, the possibility that computers become "more intelligent" than humans. We could also argue that humans and computers have different capacities (seeing structures versus fast and errorless computation) and that our approaches to solving the same problem should be completely different. Your point of view might influences whether or not you find AI dangerous, as Stephen Hawkins did for example.

Often the set of known data entries is split in a *training* and a *test set*: the algorithm is *trained* on the basis of the training set, and then evaluated on the basis of the test set. Usually an algorithm performs worse on the test set, but this is a more reliable comparison, as it avoids *overfitting*: the fact that the prediction of the algorithm is perfect for the training set but has no predictive value and therefore works bad on the test set. In statistics the terms *in sample* and *out of sample* are used for the same concepts. Understanding the background of the techniques and learning how to use them in the data science tool R is one of the main objectives of this book.

Descriptive analytics is *deductive* in nature: from the data set, we derive characterizing quantities such as means and correlations. Extending the knowledge from the training data to the whole population is *induction*. This is what we do in statistics and machine learning as part of predictive analytics. Certain predictive models combine deduction and induction: A real-life *system* is *modeled* using components. By predicting the behavior of the components (induction) we can deduce the behavior of the whole system. For example, in this way a production plant or the progression of a disease in a body can be *simulated*. By changing (the behavior of) certain components different scenarios can be analysed, leading to *optimization*, i.e., prescriptive analytics. Optimization comes in different flavors. Linear optimization is a powerful framework, used in many planning problems, such as crew scheduling in airlines and logistics. When problems are *dynamic* (e.g., they evolve over time, such as managing an investment portfolio), then *dynamic programming* is the right framework. When dynamic optimization is combined with learning, then we speak of *reinforcement learning*.

1.4   Tooling

A multitude of tools exist to assist the data analyst with his or her task. We first make a rough division between *ad hoc* and *routine* tasks. For routine tasks, standardized and often automated procedures exists for the process steps, often involving dedicated and sometimes even tailor-made software. For example:
- for data collection *data warehouses* exist with connections with operational IT systems;
- for distribution companies *decision support systems* exist that compute the optimal route of delivery trucks, saving many transit hours and petrol.

We will first go into detail on software for ad-hoc tasks. For ad-hoc tasks there are a number of proprietary and open source tools—R (open source) and *MS Excel* (proprietary) are among the most popular ones. Both allow the user to efficiently manipulate data, often represented as matrices. Each tool functions in very different ways: R manipulates data in a declarative way, very much like programming languages. Additionally, the interactive environment *RStudio* allows for an easy manipulation of data, R scripts and figures. Excel is essentially a 2-dimensional worksheet, with the possibility to perform calculations in each cell and to add entities such as figures. Both have many useful functions, for example for statistical calculation. Many libraries exist containing algorithms that can be added to these tools, both open source and proprietary. Users can also add new functions or libraries to both tools. For a screenshot of a simple implementation of linear regression in both R and Excel, see Figures 1.2 and 1.3.

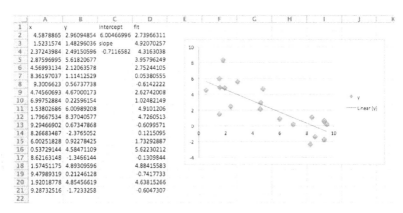

Figure 1.2: A simple implementation of linear regression in Excel

Excel is omnipresent and is easy to learn, making it the favorite tool for many people doing relatively easy computational tasks. However, Excel is also known for the errors users make with it. This might be partly due to a lack of appropriate training, but the lack of structure also contributes. R enforces more structure, just like programming languages do. Learning R requires more time but it may well be worth the investment.

As mentioned, Excel and R are both analytic environments with many built-in functions. Engines can be called from these environments to perform certain tasks, such as optimization. These engines can also be proprietary or open source. For example, for *linear optimization* (see Chapter 6), the best solvers, Gurobi and CPLEX, are proprietary; CBC is an example of an open-source solver.

Many other environments exist, often for specific analytics tasks. Examples are SPSS, often used in social sciences for statistical analysis, and

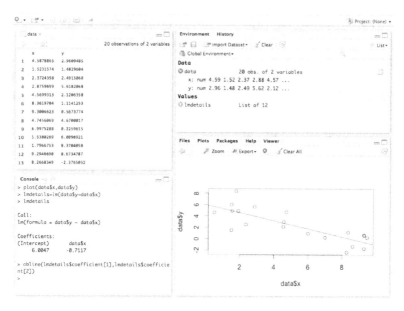

Figure 1.3: A simple implementation of linear regression in RStudio

AIMMS, an optimization environment. A special place is taken by *Python*. Python is a programming language with libraries containing many functions for data analysis. For this reason it is both used for ad hoc analysis and routine tasks, solving the so-called "two-language problem", the fact that you have to move from say R to a language like Java or C++ once you move from a successful pilot to a production system.

Excel, although very different in functionality, is also often used for routine tasks. It has some functionality for this, such as the possibility to connect to databases and to add user-friendly screens, but it lacks others, such as user management. Although in principle everything can be built within Excel, thanks to the underlying programming language VBA (*Visual Basic for Applications*), in practice it often leads to slow error-prone systems consisting of a spaghetti of multiple sheets referring to each other.

Concerning software for routine tasks, there is a large variety in possible tooling. A major difference is between *off-the-shelf* and *tailor-made* software. In the area of prescriptive analytics *decision support systems* (DSS) form the main category of off-the-shelf software. This is software built for a specific goal, such as the routing of delivery vans or the pricing of hotel rooms. Next to the analytics algorithms, DSS typically have built-in connections to data sources and allow the user to interact with the software in such a way that input and output of the algorithms can be manipulated.

In the area of data collection and descriptive analytics BI tools exist, such as IBM Cognos, that help the user collect data and execute queries. Recently, many tools are built to store and manipulate big data. Google and Amazon are major players in this area with the open-source database and data manipulation systems *Hadoop* and *Mapreduce* (mainly developed by Google) and *Amazon Web Services*, providing big data cloud storage and computing.

Tailor-made analytics software can be written in many different languages. We already mentioned Python, but popular languages include php, Java, C++ and C#, combined with mySQL (open source) or MS SQL server databases. Note the move of proprietary off-the-shelf tooling to cloud-based solutions, taking away the need for expensive servers at the customer site, and making maintenance and support much easier.

In Figure 1.4 you can find an overview of the tools discussed. In this book we will mainly use R.

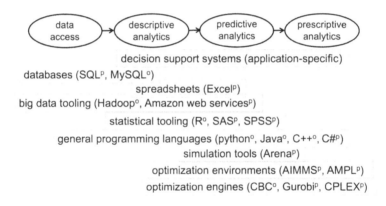

decision support systems (application-specific)
databases (SQL[p], MySQL[o])
spreadsheets (Excel[p])
big data tooling (Hadoop[o], Amazon web services[p])
statistical tooling (R[o], SAS[p], SPSS[p])
general programming languages (python[o], Java[o], C++[o], C#[p])
simulation tools (Arena[p])
optimization environments (AIMMS[p], AMPL[p])
optimization engines (CBC[o], Gurobi[p], CPLEX[p])

Figure 1.4: Types of analytics tools with some examples;
o = open source, p = proprietary

Note that many interfaces exist between the tools and languages in Figure 1.4. From within Excel and general programming languages databases can be accessed; DSS, spreadsheets and optimization environments call optimization engines, etc. Especially with the open source environments R and Python every imaginable data science project can be done, where python is preferred in the case of big data or applications requiring intensive computation. R and python are quickly gaining popularity: there is an enormous community developing new libraries and offering support through websites such as `stackoverflow.com`.

1.5   Implementation

A successful implementation of BA requires the right combination of tools
and skills from the BA consultant(s). But more is needed: the organization
should have reached the right maturity level to make the implementation
possible. Let us consider first the required skills of the specialist.

The core knowledge of any BA specialist is the command of suitable tooling (such as R) and a broad understanding of descriptive, predictive and
prescriptive methods. Next to that, a specialist might have management
skills (project management, change management, communication skills),
programming skills (in for example C++ or Python), or deep knowledge
on some of the technical areas, often clustered by the scientific disciplines
of statistics, machine learning or optimization. These specialists are considered to be "T-shaped": they have breadth and also depth in a certain area.
Sometimes people talk even of "Π-shaped", emphasizing the importance
of knowledge of the application domain, the second vertical bar. However,
the importance of breadth cannot be underestimated: It is important to be
able to use the right method for the problems one encounters. Scientists are
still too often specialized in one tool (e.g., a hammer) which they use for all
problems they encounter (e.g., to put a screw in the wall).

It is crucial to have good analysts, but an organization should also support the deployment of analytics. The extent to which an organization supports a certain concept is called its *maturity* with respect to this concept. The
maturity is measured using *maturity models*. Different analytics maturity
models have been developed. The more mature an organization, the higher
the impact of analytics. We illustrate the concept using the "INFORMS Analytics Maturity Model" [1]. It consists of three sets of questions, concerning
the organization, its analytics capability, and its data and infrastructure. On
the basis of this a score is calculated. For example, an organization with a
central data warehouse and a centralized analytics strategy will score higher
than a company lacking these.

1.6   Additional reading

General information on many subjects can be found on Wikipedia. We already mentioned Davenport & Harris [8], which is still an interesting non-
technical book to read on the value of BA.

For more background on errors in Excel see Powell et al. [29] and other

---
Box 1.3. Legal and ethical aspects

Although not his or her main focus, a data scientist should be aware of legal and ethical aspects. The legal aspects often start with the data collection: are you allowed to get and analyze the data? Some form of *data anonymization* can be useful in this process. Current laws (such as the EU GDPR regulation) also limit the amount of time you are allowed to keep data, which contradicts the wish to keep as much data as possible for future analysis.

There are many privacy issues that have to do with data, like who has access to data about you, who owns it, and how do you know which data is out there about you? Ethical questions also arise around the use of algorithms. On what basis do algorithms make decisions about for example employment? Algorithms can be discriminating because they were trained to do so by the data. On the other hand, a data science approach can also give solutions, for example by communicating all parameters of a predictive model.

---

papers by the same authors.

Some interesting ideas on the different profiles of data scientists (on which part of Section 1.5 is based) can be found in Harris et al. [14].

More information on project management can be found in Klastorin [21]. A classic on change management is Kotter [22].

You can try the INFORMS Analytics Maturity Model yourself at [1].

A well-know mathematician and author writing on ethical issues of data science is Cathy O'Neil, see for example her TED talks and [27].

Chapter 2

Going on a Tour with R

In this chapter we introduce a number of fundamental BA methods while introducing the tool R. The goal is not to teach you as much as possible of R, but to give you enough basic understanding that you can find the information you need to solve a certain problem yourself.

Learning outcomes   On completion of this chapter, you will be able to:

- use R and RStudio for simple calculations

- reflect on the possibilities of R

- obtain additional knowledge of R and extend your R skills

2.1   Getting started

First download install R and then RStudio (in that order). You can find the right links by searching the internet for "download R" and "download RStudio". When you start RStudio (as in Figure 1.3) it has a "console" window at the bottom left with a ">" prompt. After the prompt type commands that you finish with "Enter". R can be seen as a system for matrix manipulation with additional analytics functionality. First explore the basic functionality by, for example, typing the following commands:

```
> 3+4
> sqrt(3^2+4^2)
> x=1:10; sqrt(2*x)
```

```
> y=2*1:10; x*y
> sum(x*y)
> plot(x,y)
```

You will see that the variables we defined can be found in the "environment" window on the top right. Here you can also import datasets and clear all variables. Another possibility is the use of the `rm()` function:

```
> rm(x); x
```

The figures appear in the lower right window. When you load or write a script a new window appears in the top left corner. This way you can edit, save and execute a series of commands. This is essential when working on a project or when sharing your R scripts. There is also a shortcut to execute commands from the script window in the console (Cmd-Enter on a Mac).

It is very important to be able to load data from a file. The simplest way is through the "Import Dataset" wizard in the top-right environment window. As an exercise, open a blank workbook in Excel, enter some random numbers from cell `A1` downward and use `Save as...` to save it as a `csv` file, let's say with the name `Book1.csv`. Open this file in R with the "Import Dataset" wizard. This will create a *data frame* `Book1` with a (default) column `V1`. You can now manipulate the data, for example by entering:

```
> mean(Book1$V1)
```

or

```
> mean(Book1[,1])
```

You can also first assign the numbers to a vector:

```
> x=Book1$V1; x; x[1]; x[1:10]; mean(x)
```

Note that R follows many computer programming conventions: arguments are between brackets (such as `mean(x)`); vector or matrix cells are between square brackets (such as `x[1]`); commands on the same line are separated by a semi-colon, etc. Programmers definitely have an advantage when using R, but non-programmers will also quickly get the hang of it.

At some point, you might want to enter data directly from the console, for example as part of a script in which you routinely load new data. You first need RStudio to point to the right folder. For this you need the commands `getwd()` and `setwd()` (get and set working directory). After that, you can load the data using a command such as `read.table`. Looking at the console output of the wizard will help you get started. Help can be obtained through `help(read.table)`. For other input formats such as Excel, there are versatile *libraries* to customise the input.

2.2 Learning R

This chapter is not meant as a tutorial, but to give you a quick start to R and to help you avoid certain pitfalls. There are many books written on R, but because of all the free resources available in R itself and on the internet, there is no real need to buy one. Within R the function `help(topic)` or `?topic` will give you help on the topic entered. The information provided is complete, however it is sometimes hard to understand. More accessible information can often be found on the internet, usually by searching for "R topic". Also, more tutorial-type webpages exist on many different topics. For example, when you search Google for "R data frame" you get 192M hits, the first ones being very simple tutorials on this important subject. For more advanced topics, you are best helped via online communities such as `stackoverflow.com`.

Also very helpful are *cheat sheets*, which exist for R as well as for many *libraries* as discussed in the next section. You can find them by googling for "R cheat sheet".

2.3   Libraries

Today, scientists not only write papers on their latest algorithms, but they also publish *R libraries* in which they are implemented. This implicates that the tooling available in R expands rapidly and that it exceeds many of the commercial tools by far. Libraries exist for many different algorithms—from traditional forecasting algorithms to modern deep learning algorithms—but also for non-algorithmic tasks. Examples of the latter category are `ggplot` for making graphically attractive plots or `shiny` for making R interactive. A very simple example with `ggplot` is as follows:

```
> install.packages("ggplot2")     # install package (once)
> library(ggplot2)                # load package
> x=sample(6,100,replace=TRUE)    # draw 100 times from a die
> qplot(x, geom="histogram")      # plot using ggplot
```

Note that everything following the "#"-sign is interpreted by R as comments.

2.4   Data structures

Crucial to R is an understanding of data types. Variables in R can be numbers, logical values, strings of characters, or dates, just like in other programming languages. Typical values are

```
> number=3.14; logical=TRUE; string="hello"
```

You can check the type by using the `typeof()` function. Assigning dates is a bit more complex:

```
> date = as.Date("2002-01-27")
```

Exercise 2.1 *Compute the number of days since you were born, using an appropriate built-in function to get today's date. Do the same for the number of seconds. Do not round to days. The R functions* `as.double` *and* `strptime` *might come in handy.*

Vectors can be constructed in a number of ways. Examples are:

```
> rep("x",10); c(2,5,-1); (1:10)^2
```

From vectors you can make *lists*, *matrices*, and *data frames*. Lists are the most versatile: it is a list of vectors, possibly of different lengths. Matrices are the most restrictive: the vectors need to have the same length, implying that a matrix has rows and columns, and all values are the same type. However, the data structure you will use most often is a data frame. In a data frame, all vectors have the same length, just as for matrices, but the columns can contain different types of values. Typically, the rows represent the elements or samples of your data, and the columns the attributes. For example, with

```
> df = data.frame(c("Ali","Bo","Cor","Di"),c("m","f","m","f"),
c(23,27,33,17))
```

you create a data frame with 4 rows and 3 columns. With

```
> colnames(df) = c("name","sex","age")
```

you can give appropriate names to the columns. There are many useful commands to view and manipulate the data, such as:

```
> df[[2]]; df[,2]; df[,-2]; df$sex; df[1,]; levels(df$sex)
> mean(df$age); df[df$sex=="f",]; tapply(df$age,df$sex,mean)
```

Exercise 2.2 *Create a data frame with names, birthdays and sex of a number of friends or family. Write R commands to add an attribute "age" in years, to compute the average age of men and women, and to find the names of the youngest man and woman.*

Note that in practice, we rarely create data frames as we usually import them. Often we have to apply functions like as.integer to convert the entries to the appropriate type.

2.5   Programming

Basic use of R involves calling, sometimes nested, 1-line commands such as df$name[which.max(df$age)], which gives the name of the oldest person in the data frame. Sometimes the use of standard functions is not sufficient to do a complex operation, and conditions and loops (similar to other programming languages) are required. An example, containing both and if and a for-statement, is as follows:

```
> df$cat = NA
> for(p in 1:length(df)){if(df$age[p]<18){
+    df$cat[p]="minor"}else{df$cat[p]="adult"}
```

Lengthy R scripts might become hard to read. Sometimes we want to repeat the same piece multiple times, or even call it from different scripts. In these cases, new *functions* can be made. Suppose you often need the average of the minimum and the maximum of a vector. Then you can write the following function:

```
> my_func = function(x) {return((max(x)+min(x))/2)}
```

When executed by R, it gives no output, but from now on it is available anytime. An example of its use is as follows:

```
> v=(1:10)^2; my_func(v)
```

The proper use of these aspects of R requires programming experience and knowledge about conventions to build good code. These can be obtained as part of an R course, but more often it is part of a programming course for a language such as Java or Python.

Now we will discuss two more ways to extend the functionality of R. The first is *R Markdown*. It is an easy way to make a report in which text, R code and the outcomes are integrated. An example can be found in Figure 2.1. There is an online cheat sheet to help you get started.

Figure 2.1: An example of R Markdown

Interactive web applications can be built with the package *shiny*. Your first shiny app can easily be made by opening a new shiny document within Rstudio and then following the instructions. An example can be found in Figure 2.2.

2.6   Simulation and hypothesis testing

Next we briefly show how some typical data science tasks can be done using R, starting with hypothesis testing.

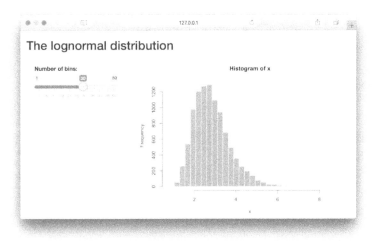

Figure 2.2: An example of an interactive shiny app

As we saw, rolling a die 100 times can be executed by the following command:

```
> x=sample(6,100,replace=TRUE); x
```

This is in fact *simulation*: we simulated the roll of a die 100 times. To understand the command and to see what other arguments can be given, use:

```
> ?sample
```

Calculating its mean and plotting a histogram is done as follows:

```
> mean(x); hist(x)
```

As a simple example of hypothesis testing, suppose we want to check the fairness of a coin. We toss the coin 100 times and heads comes up 55 times. Is this strong evidence that our coin is unfair or should we stick for the moment to the *null hypothesis* that the coin is fair? To answer this question, we have to find out how likely 55 is as an outcome under the null hypothesis. In the previous century, mathematicians developed formulae to answer this type of question. Today, we can use computers to get a more insightful method which consists of simulating the 100 tosses. To simulate the 100 tosses in one time, use `rbinom(1,100,0.5)`. The outcome is the number of times heads comes up. Entering "up" and "Enter" multiple times in the console window makes R repeat the experiment. To simulate the 100 tosses 1000 times and store it in the variable `exp` use `exp=rbinom(1000,100,0.5)`.

We are now interested in the likelihood of an outcome of 55 *or more extreme* under the null hypothesis. `sum(exp>=55)` counts the number of occurences of 55 or higher in the simulation. The answer depends on the initial value of the random number generator (which can be set by `set.seed()`), but is likely around 180. This means that in 18% of the experiments the outcome is 55 or higher. This number is called the *p-value*. 18% is not considered to be low enough to reject the null hypothesis, i.e., the fact that the outcome is higher than the expected 50 might very well be due to randomness in the coin tossing experiment.

R contains functions for all standard hypothesis tests. In the current situation the call is `binom.test(55,n=100,p=0.5,alt="g")`. The last part of the call (`alt="g"`) has to do with the fact that the test is *one-sided*. As part of the output we find indeed that the *p*-value is close to 18%. (In fact, in the current situation it makes more sense to perform a two-sided test. Then the *p*-value becomes 36%.)

2.7   Clustering

+---+
| **Box 2.1. Resetting the random number generator** |
| If you want to obtain exactly the same results as reported below, start with |
| `set.seed(0)` and execute the commands in exactly the same order. The func- |
| tion `set.seed()` is useful when debugging: it resets the random number gen- |
| erator and allows you to reproduce results obtained earlier. |
+---+

To illustrate clustering we make a data set with 100 data points and 6 clusters by throwing a die again. We define a matrix which we fill as follows: the first column contains the die rolls, the second and third column gives a cluster per outcome plus some random noise:

```
> x=matrix(,nrow=100,ncol=3)
> x[,1]=sample(6,100,replace=TRUE)
> x[,2]=rnorm(100,(x[,1]+1)%/%2,0.15)
> x[,3]=rnorm(100,(x[,1]+1)%%2,0.15)
```

Without the `norm` (the random noise), there would only be 6 different points. The exact meaning of these R commands will become clear in the next chapter. For now what matters is the output, in the second and third column, visualized by the dots with > `plot(x[,-1])` in Figure 2.3.

A popular clustering algorithm is *k-means*. It can be executed and immediately plotted, with 6 centers, using the following command:

```
> points(kmeans(x[,-1],6)$centers,pch=3,cex=1.5)
```

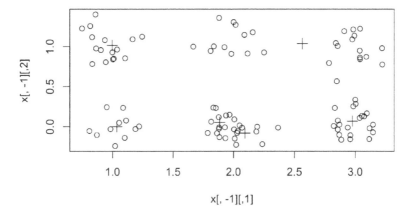

Figure 2.3: An example with 6 clusters

It is visible as plusses in Figure 2.3. What is remarkable is that the algorithm did not find the logical clusters: it places two centers in one cluster and then sees the two upper-right clusters as one. Repeating the algorithm without resetting the seed (see Box 2.1) gives different results. This is typical for many machine learning algorithms: there is no quality guarantee for the outcome, and a lot of fine tuning often needs to be done. The good news is that there are many computational methods to evaluate the quality of outcomes. Essential in this situation are good quality measures, by which we can compare solutions. Obviously, they also depend on the goal of the algorithm. A common objective in clustering is to minimize the sum of the squared differences of each point to the center of the cluster to which it belongs.

2.8 Regression and deep learning

Regression analysis is the somewhat inappropriate name for a class of problems in which there is a target value that we have to approximate. The most common one is *linear regression*. Assume in the data set that we just constructed, that we want to approximate the value of the die rolls. We say that the first column of the data set x[,1] is *explained* by the x[,2] and x[,3]. In R we call the linear model in the following way:

```
> lm(x[,1]~x[,2]+x[,3])
```

It gives as output the *statistical model* $-0.84 + 1.94$ x[,2] $+ 0.94$ x[,3] which predicts the values quite well. This works well also for other values than 1,...,6, as can be seen in Figure 2.4 for the six centers of the clusters and the points (4,0) and (4,1).

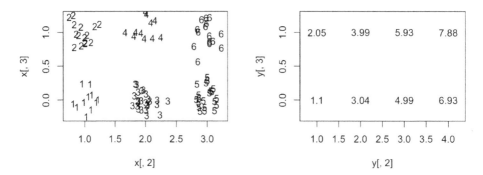

Figure 2.4: An example of regression: data on the left, predictions on the right

A regression technique that has gained enormous popularity recently and that works especially well for unstructured data such as text or images, is *artificial neural networks* (ANNs) with multiple layers, known under the name of *deep learning*. For the purpose of illustration, we made the relations non-linear, as you can see in the left graph of Figure 2.5: the 1s and 2s lie closer together than the 5s and 6s. The linear model just used does not work well on this data. Although some adaptations to the linear model could be done (for more on this, see Section 4.3), we will use another method, neural networks. The data and results are in Figure 2.5 and the neural network itself is in Figure 2.6. The non-linearities can be seen in the right-hand side figure: for example, for y[,2] equal to 1, we see the y[,3] value increasing from 0.98 to 1.94 and then stay at that value. This is clearly non-linear.

Successful implementations of deep learning for applications such as image recognition contain many intermediate *hidden* layers with possibly thousands of parameters. They require a lot of fine tuning from the engineers who build them and quite some computational power to determine the parameters. Once this *learning* is done the algorithm can be quickly run to analyse new images.

2.9   Classification

Now let's assume that you're not interested in the values of x[,1], but you want to find the 6s. In that case, we want to approximate the logi-

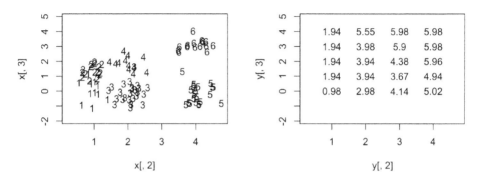

Figure 2.5: An example of an ANN: data on the left, predictions on the right

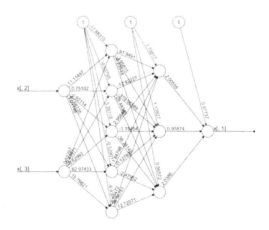

Figure 2.6: An example of an ANN: the network itself

cal (true/false) values in Figure 2.7. There are many algorithms to do this, amongst which an extension of linear regression (*logistic regression*) and deep learning. Here we use a different technique: *decision trees*. We can use the following R code, leading to the tree of the right figure of Figure 2.7. The package requires a data frame, thus we first transform x into a data frame, which now has column names such as z$V1. We make our new dataset by recalculating the first column and then we call the rpart function:

```
> z=as.data.frame(x)
> z$V1=(z$V1==6)
> library(rpart)
> rpart(V1~V2+V3,data=z,method="class")
```

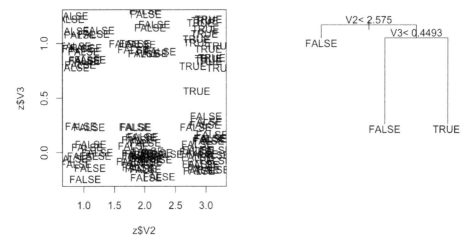

Figure 2.7: An example of a decision tree: data on the left, the tree on the right

We see how the tree classifies: values with $V2 \geq 2.575$ and $V3 \geq 0.4493$, the upper-right corner, are classified as true.

2.10   Optimization

Suppose that, for example using regression, you have found how certain features influence a certain target value. Some features are under your control, and you want to maximize (or minimize) the target value. The question to answer is: how to set the controllable features?

As an example, suppose that you studied how different people with a certain disease react to different mixtures of medication. For a new patient the question would be: what are the optimal doses?

When the number of possibilities is small (e.g., drug A or B in a few specific doses) then we can solve this problem by *enumeration*, which is simply trying all possibilities. When we can vary the doses, or even change a mixture, then we need an algorithm to find the optimal solution.

As an example, suppose we can use 2 types of medication, at a price of 10 and 15 Euros/mg. For a particular patient, the following holds: if only drug 1 is used 30 mg is required, but you can mix it with drug 2, which is twice as effective. However, to avoid adverse effects, you cannot administer more than 10 mg of drug 2. What is the cheapest combination satisfying the constraints? This *linear optimization* problem can be solved using the lpsolve package. Let x_1 be the amount of drug of type 1 and x_2 the amount of type 2. Then we want to minimize $10x_1 + 15x_2$ under the constraints $x_1 + 2x_2 \geq 30$ and $x_2 \leq 10$. In R this can be entered as follows:

```
> library(lpSolve)
> objective = c(10,15)
> constraints = matrix(c(1,2,0,1),nrow=2,byrow=TRUE)
> directions = c(">=","<=")
> rhs = c(30,10)
> lp("min",objective,constraints,directions,rhs)$solution
```

Perhaps you could have solved this problem by hand, but this method allows for thousands of variables and constraints, problems for which an efficient algorithm is absolutely necessary.

2.11 Additional reading

R Markdown (the tool by which we made the report of Figure 2.1) uses the markup language Markdown, for which documentation is amply available on the internet.

The subjects of each of the sections are discussed in more details in the corresponding chapters. At the end of each chapter pointers to relevant literature are given.

Chapter 3

Variability

Variability is omnipresent: without variability every moment of the day would be the same. Often there is a certain level of uncertainty about variability: we do know exactly when it is light and dark, but we do not know exactly when it will rain. Data science tries to explain, predict and control the variability we observe. The study of variability is therefore crucial for a solid understanding of data science and business analytics. This goes beyond studying the data itself: mathematical theory helps us understand the data and obtain results about the data. Mathematics and statistics impose a theoretical framework in which, under well-specified conditions, certain results are obtained. When these conditions are (approximately) verified in the data, then we can use the mathematical results, which makes us understand our data much better.

In this chapter we focus on univariate data and models. We first show how to summarize data. If you have data on all items you are interested in then this might be sufficient. However, often you only have data on part of the *population*. Or, you want to predict future values of the data based on historical values. In this case you need to be able to distinguish between *noise* and *signal*: is the summary representative of the population or is there so much noise that a new experiment would give very different results? Do we *overfit* our data such that our prediction has little predictive value? To answer these types of questions, we will apply basic probability theory, especially distributions and the central limit theorem. After that, we introduce some useful hypothesis tests. This closes the circle: using results from probability theory we draw conclusions from data.

This chapter is more mathematical in nature than most others. You can always skip certain parts and move on to the next chapter.

Learning outcomes   On completion of this chapter, you will be able to:

- describe the basic notions of probability, descriptive statistics and hypothesis testing

- summarize data using R

- perform basic calculations by hand and in R related to distributions, confidence intervals and hypothesis testing

- understand the sources of variability in business data

3.1   Summarizing data

Data can be summarized in numerical and graphical ways. For univariate, i.e., 1-dimensional data, numerical summaries mostly concentrate on *centrality* and *variability*. The most common measure for centrality is the mean (mean() in R, also called average), equal to the sum of the values divided by the number. Other measures for centrality are the trimmed mean (by adding a second argument to the mean() function) and the median (median()). The trimmed mean ignores the lowest and highest values, the median is the "middle" value, for which 50% is lower and 50% is higher.

For variability we mostly use the standard deviation (SD, sd() in R) or the variance (var, the square of the SD). They are defined later, but for both hold: the higher the value, the higher the variability.

For example, the R datasets package contains a number of datasets of which eurodist is one. It contains distances (in km) between a number of major European cities. Then the R commands
```
> mean(eurodist); mean(eurodist,trim=0.1); median(eurodist)
> sd(eurodist); var(eurodist)
```
result in: 1505.1, 1422.9, 1311.5, 898.8 and 807813. Note that the second command computes the trimmed mean, ignoring the 10% lowest and highest values.

Exercise 3.1 *Reproduce this calculation (you might need to load the* datasets *library). Do the same thing for a dataset consisting of all the same numbers. You can construct such a dataset with the function* rep()*. Now change a few of the numbers and look at the consequences.*

> **Box 3.1. The use of the mean**
> Very often we are interested in the average. However, this average might be highly influenced by a number of extreme points.
> For example, you might be interested in the average price of houses in a certain area, and see how it evolves over time. In many neighborhoods, this average is highly influenced by a small number of very expensive luxury houses. If you are interested in the price of a common house then the trimmed mean or the median might be a better choice.

Next we consider graphical summaries, especially *histograms* and *box-plots*, made using the R functions `hist()` and `boxplot()`. Output for the `eurodist` dataset can be found in Figure 3.1. A histogram has different values grouped in buckets (here of length 500) on the horizontal axis and their frequencies on the vertical axis. We see, for example, that values between 1000 and 1500 km occur 52 times. A box plot is common in statistics and is essentially a 1-dimensional diagram in which the box is limited by the first and third quartile of the data (i.e., the points with 25% and 75% of the data below them, in R `quantile(eurodist,0.25)` and `quantile(eurodist,0.75)`), with the second quartile (the median) in the middle. There are different definitions for the horizontal lines (the *whiskers*) but the idea is that they show dispersion. Data points outside of the whiskers, the *outliers*, are shown as small circles.

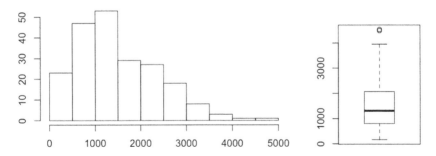

Figure 3.1: Histogram and boxplot

Regardless of your ultimate goal, it is always good to start with summarizing your data. This helps you to get a general impression of the data, its outliers, *skewness*, etc.

Exercise 3.2 *Use the* `AirPassengers` *dataset from the* `datasets` *package. Com-*

Box 3.2. Skewness and outliers

From the example we see that the dataset is not symmetric, but *skewed* to the right with two *outliers* beyond 4000. This skewness to the right results in a mean that is bigger than the median. The outliers make the SD high.

Data is rarely symmetric. Only in certain cases theory predicts symmetry, in other cases we hardly ever find it.

Box 3.3. Summarizing data in Excel

Functions in Excel have partly different names than in R: average, median, percentile, stdev, and var. To construct a histogram you can use the "data analysis" add-in, which is unfortunately not available in all versions of Excel. You can also make the histogram by hand, by calculating first the number of data points per bucket, as illustrated in the example below.

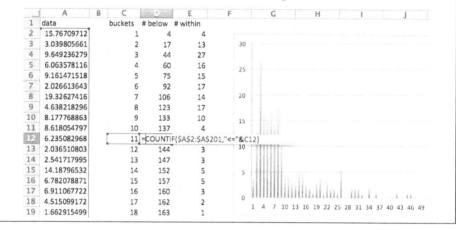

---

pute all 5 quartiles, the average and the SD. Plot the histogram and the boxplot. You can do this in R and/or in Excel.

3.2 Probability theory and the binomial distribution

In the previous section we analyzed data, which might be useful by itself. However, we might also consider the data to be outcomes of some experiment with uncertain, random outcomes. What can we say of the experiment on the basis of its outcomes? How can we define the experiment in a useful way? Probability theory gives the framework to answer this type of question. In probability, a random experiment is called a *random variable* (RV), often denoted with the letter X. An RV X is different from a regular variable x

in the sense that it can take multiple values, according to its *distribution*. For example, if X models the rolling of a die then it can take values $\{1, 2, \ldots, 6\}$, each with probability $1/6$.

Distributions come in two flavors: *discrete* and *continuous*. Discrete RVs can take a finite or *countable* number of values. For example, rolling a die (with possible outcomes $1, \ldots, 6$), flipping a coin (0 or 1), or the number of arrivals to a service center (possibly $0, 1, 2, \ldots$).

Continuous RVs can take any value within a specified range, for example all values positive and negative (denoted by $\mathbb{R}$), only positive values ($\mathbb{R}^+$), or a range such as $[1, 5]$, the interval from 1 to 5. Examples are body heights and GDP of a country.

In what follows, we discuss a number of often used distributions, starting with discrete ones. We start with the *Bernoulli* and *binomial* distributions. While discussing them we introduce some important concepts from probability theory.

The Bernoulli distribution The Bernoulli distribution (named after the Swiss mathematician) can only take two values: 0 and 1. It models situations such as coin tossing. Random variables always have numbers as outcomes, therefore in the cointossing case "heads" and "tails" are translated to 0 and 1. A Bernoulli distributed RV X is completely defined by the probability p by which 1 occurs, written as $\mathbb{P}(X = 1) = p$, which should be read as "the probability that the RV X is equal to 1 is equal to p".

A common way to plot a distribution is by its *cumulative distribution function* (cdf), usually denoted as $F(x)$ or $F_X(x)$, and defined as $F_X(x) = \mathbb{P}(X \leq x)$. It follows that F is a non-decreasing function with $F(-\infty) = 0$ and $F(\infty) = 1$. When X is continuous F is also continuous (hence the name). When X is discrete, F is a *step function*: it is constant between the values that can occur and at these points it makes jumps. F_X for X Bernoulli is plotted in Figure 3.2.

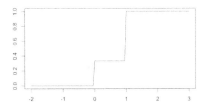

Figure 3.2: The cdf of the Bernoulli distribution

Exercise 3.3 *For the cdf below, give the possible outcomes and their probabilities.*

In a way somewhat similar to the mean of a dataset, we can compute the *expectation* of a random variable: it is an average over all possible outcomes, weighted with the probabilities.

Example 3.1 *Rolling a die has as possible outcomes $1, \ldots, 6$, each with probability $1/6$. Its expectation is therefore $\frac{1}{6} \times (1 + \cdots + 6) = 3.5$.*

In a similar way we can also compute the SD and variance of a RV. They are denoted as $\mathbb{E}X$, $\sigma(X)$, and $\sigma^2(X)$, respectively. For the Bernoulli distribution their values are:

$$\mathbb{E}X = p, \quad \sigma(X) = \sqrt{p(1-p)}, \quad \sigma^2(X) = p(1-p). \tag{3.1}$$

Box 3.4. Mathematical expectation and variance

The definition of the expectation for a discrete RV X is as follows:

$$\mathbb{E}X = \sum_{x: \, \mathbb{P}(X=x)>0} x\mathbb{P}(X = x).$$

For X Bernoulli this gives $\mathbb{E}X = 0\mathbb{P}(X = 0) + 1\mathbb{P}(X = 1) = p$. The variance is the expected quadratic difference from the expectation:

$$\sigma^2(X) = \mathbb{E}(X - \mathbb{E}X)^2 = \sum_{x: \, \mathbb{P}(X=x)>0} (x - \mathbb{E}X)^2 \mathbb{P}(X = x).$$

For X Bernoulli it is $\sigma^2(X) = (0 - p)^2(1 - p) + (1 - p)^2 p = p - p^2$.

The Bernoulli distribution is a special case of the binomial distribution, which we will discuss next. R functions for both distributions will be introduced after that.

The binomial distribution   Suppose we repeat a $0/1$ experiment n times. We assume that they are *independent*, meaning that the outcome of one does not influence another. Let N be the total number of 1s. Then N has a so-called *binomial* distribution. The binomial distribution has two parameters: the success probability p, and n. For $n = 10$ and $p = 0.2$ its cdf is plotted in Figure 3.3. This plot was made using the following R command: `curve(pbinom(x,10,0.2))`.

Box 3.5. Independence

Independence is a very important property. Often we repeat an experiment multiple times. For example, we try a new medication on multiple patients, or we observe multiple visitors to a webshop. Statistical independence states that the outcome of one experiment does not influence the other. We assume it quite often, because it makes the analysis much simpler, although it might not be completely true. For example, a webshop customer who purchased a product might leave a positive review, thereby increasing the purchase probability of future customers. In this situation, the experiments are not independent, although the purchase probability might have only changed very little.

However, there are situations where we prefer not to have independence. For example, if we know the cancer type of each patient and the effect of a certain medication, then we might hope for dependence, i.e., a correlation between the type of cancer and the effect, in order to be able to give the right medication to the right patient. Similarly, you hope that *attributes* such as previous visits, age, time on website, etc., influence the conversion probability in order to be able to steer behavior of webshop visitors, for example by targeted advertising. These are typical examples of multivariate problems which we will discuss in later chapters.

The name binomial comes from Newton's *binomium*, written as $\binom{n}{k}$. It gives the number of ways to select k items out of n, is related to the *Triangle of Pascal*, and is part of the formula for $\mathbb{P}(N = k)$. We will not go into the mathematical details, instead we discuss the R functions by which we can compute expressions such as $\mathbb{P}(N = k)$, the probability of k successes. There are 4 R functions:

- `dbinom(k, n, p)`, which gives $\mathbb{P}(N = k)$ for parameters n and p;
- `pbinom(k, n, p)`, which gives $\mathbb{P}(N \leq k)$ for parameters n and p;
- `rbinom(k, n, p)`, which gives k random independent outcomes of N with parameters n and p;
- `qbinom(q, n, p)`, which gives the *inverse* of the cdf: the number k such that $\mathbb{P}(N \leq k)$ is equal or just above q.

As an example, consider a school class with 30 kids who are randomly

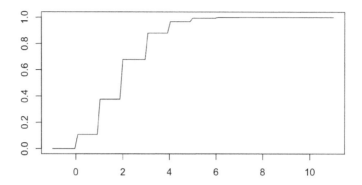

Figure 3.3: The cdf of the binomial distribution with $n = 10$ and $p = 0.2$

selected. We assume that the probability of every child being male or fe-
male is exactly 50%. Then the probability of having 15 kids of each sex is
dbinom(15,30,0.5) is equal to 14.4%. Having 10 or less girls has probability pbinom(10,30,0.5), 5%.

Generating 10 arbitrary classes by rbinom(10,30,0.5) leads to: 18 13 13
12 15 16 14 14 19 17.

Explaining the use of qbinom() is a bit harder. Suppose we want to
know the maximum number of girls to expect in 90% of the classes. Then
qbinom(0.9,30,0.5) gives the answer: 19. Indeed, pbinom(19,30,0.5) $=$
$\mathbb{P}(N \leq 19) \geq 0.9$ and pbinom$(18,30,0.5) = \mathbb{P}(N \leq 18) < 0.9$.

The values given by qbinom() are also called *percentiles*. The 25th, 50th
and 75th percentile are called *quartiles*; the 50th percentile is the median of
the distribution.

Exercise 3.4 *You roll a die 10 times. What is the probability that there are no 6s?
Make a plot of the probability of k 6s for $k \in \{0, \ldots, 10\}$.*

Note that the R functions for the binomial distribution can be used as
well for the Bernoulli distribution, by taking $n = 1$.

The formulas for the expectation, SD and variance are as follows:

$$\mathbb{E}N = np, \quad \sigma(N) = \sqrt{np(1-p)}, \quad \sigma^2(N) = np(1-p).$$

Note the resemblance with the Bernoulli distribution. The reason for this is
explained hereafter.

Example 3.2 *You roll a die 10 times. Then you expect* $10 \times \frac{1}{6} = 1.67$ *times a 6, and the standard deviation of the number of 6s is* $\sqrt{10 \times \frac{1}{6} \times \frac{5}{6}} = 1.18$.

Sums of independent random variables Often we are interested in sums or averages of usually independent random variables. We will discuss two aspects of this: the distribution of sums and the expectation and SD of sums and averages. Let us start with the latter. For random variables, the following rules hold:
- the expectation of the sum is the sum of the expectations;
- the expectation of a constant times a RV is the constant times the expectation.

In mathematical terms this is equivalent to:

$$\mathbb{E}(X + Y) = \mathbb{E}X + \mathbb{E}Y \quad \text{and} \quad \mathbb{E}(cX) = c\mathbb{E}X.$$

The first formula explains why $\mathbb{E}N = n\mathbb{E}X$ for N binomial and X Bernoulli. It is interesting to note that X and Y do not even have to be independent!.

Example 3.3 *X and Y denote next year's profit of two business units of a company. The total expected profit is $\mathbb{E}X + \mathbb{E}Y$. X and Y are allowed to be dependent, for example on the same yet unknown interest rate.*

Business unit 1 has to pay 30% taxes. Its expected tax payment is $0.3\mathbb{E}X$.

For the SD and the variance things are a bit more complicated:
- the variance of the sum is the sum of the variances;
- the SD of a constant times the RV is the constant times the SD.

In mathematical terms:

$$\sigma^2(X + Y) = \sigma^2(X) + \sigma^2(Y) \quad \text{and} \quad \sigma(cX) = c\sigma(X).$$

Here X and Y need to be independent (in fact, *uncorrelated* suffices). Because $\sigma(X) = \sqrt{\sigma^2(X)}$ and $\sigma^2(X) = (\sigma(X))^2$ we also have:

$$\sigma(X + Y) = \sqrt{\sigma^2(X) + \sigma^2(Y)} \quad \text{and} \quad \sigma^2(cX) = c^2\sigma^2(X).$$

Example 3.4 *We continue with Example 3.3. Suppose that the numbers are as follows: $\mathbb{E}X = 8$, $\sigma(X) = 3$, $\mathbb{E}Y = 12$, $\sigma(Y) = 4$ (all in M€). Let us assume that X and Y are independent. Then $\mathbb{E}(X + Y) = 20$ and*

$$\sigma(X + Y) = \sqrt{3^2 + 4^2} = 5,$$

which is considerably smaller than the sums of the SDs, which is 7. This is exactly why investors "spread" their risk: the risk of a portfolio is smaller than the sum of the risks. The loss on one investment might be compensated by the others.

The caveat is in the independence: in times of economic downturn the values of assets tend all to go down contradicting the independence.

Thus, in these expressions it is crucial not to replace SD by variance and vice versa! The mathematical proofs of all expressions are not very difficult but require some experience with manipulating summations and integrals.

Averages   Let us now consider averages. To do so, let $X_1, \ldots, X_n$ be n independent RVs with the same distribution. Thus they have the same expectation and SD. Define $\overline{X}$ as the average of $X_1, \ldots, X_n$:

$$\overline{X} = \frac{X_1 + \cdots + X_n}{n}. \tag{3.2}$$

Averages play an extremely important role in statistics, because for high n they tend to the expectation, as we will see below. Therefore averages are used as estimators in cases where the expectation is unknown. We give the expectation and SD of the average:

$$\mathbb{E}\overline{X} = \mathbb{E}X_1 \quad \text{and} \quad \sigma(\overline{X}) = \sigma(X_1)/\sqrt{n}. \tag{3.3}$$

Exercise 3.5 *Verify the correctness of these expressions using the rules presented earlier.*

How should we interpret these results? Our (statistical) experiment consists of n observations. The outcome is likely (in the statistical sense: with high probability) to be close to the expectation. As we perform more observations, then the outcome is likely to be closer to the expectation: the SD decreases, because we divide by $\sqrt{n}$. Note that the function $\sqrt{n}$ increases slowly, therefore if we want to increase the accuracy of the outcome, we have to include many more observations! When we perform infinitely many observations (a mathematical abstraction, we cannot perform that many observations in practice) then the SD becomes 0 and we find exactly the expectation.

This result is known as the **law of large numbers** (LLN). It is the basis of statistics: if we take a sufficiently large sample from a population then the average is a reliable estimator of the expectation. In the context of hypothesis testing, we will discuss when a sample is "sufficiently large". Note that it is assumed that all observations have the same distribution and are independent. In the design of an experiment, this means that there is no *selection bias*, every observation should be representative for the whole population.

Exercise 3.6 *Sample 1000 times from a Bernoulli distribution with success probability 0.5. For every n, take the average over the first n numbers and make a plot of this as a function of n. How does this illustrate the LLN?*

Sometimes we are interested in the distribution of a sum of distributions. This is for example the case if we roll a die twice and we want to know the probability that the sum of the outcomes is 10. In such a case there are multiple approaches:
- in certain cases we have theoretical results concerning sums. The binomial distribution is an excellent illustration of this: it is itself a sum of Bernoulli distributions having the same p, and for the same reason sums of binomial distributions are again binomial, a long as they are independent and have the same p. Another example is the normal distribution, which will be discussed later on: sums of normals are again normal;
- for the majority of sums no mathematical expression is known. In that case we can often do a numerical calculation to compute the *joint* distribution;
- a simple and intuitive alternative is *sampling* or *simulation*, based on the LLN. You simply sample every component of the sum many times and you take the sums. For example, `rbinom(100,20,0.2)+rbinom(100,10,0.2)` gives 100 samples of a binomial distribution with parameters 30 and 0.2. If you change one of the ps the sum is not binomial anymore. However, the method can still be used.

Exercise 3.7 *a. Simulate the sum of two dice many times and use this to approximate the probability that the sum of the outcomes is 10.*
b. Determine the probability by calculating all possible outcomes that lead to 10 and their probabilities.

3.3   Other distributions and the central limit theorem

In the previous section we introduced the binomial distribution and used it to introduce some important concepts from probability theory. In this section we introduce some other well-known distributions.

The Poisson distribution   The Poisson distribution is used in practice to model customer arrivals to service centers, such as visits to web sites or calls to a call center. Arrivals to these centers show fluctuations from minute to minute. Statistical analysis shows that they often follow a Poisson distribution.

The Poisson distribution (named after the French mathematician who invented it) has a single parameter, often indicated with the Greek letter λ. A Poisson distributed RV N has the special property that $\mathbb{E}N = \sigma^2(N) = \lambda$. Sums of Poisson distributions are again Poisson distributions with the sum of the parameters.

Exercise 3.8 *For a fixed λ, consider binomial distributions N_n with n experiments and success probability λ/n. Look up the formula for the binomial distribution (e.g., at Wikipedia) and show that $\lim_{n\to\infty} \mathbb{P}(N_n = k)$ equals the Poisson distribution. (This exercise requires knowledge of calculus, the mathematical field that includes integration and limits.)*

The R functions for the Poisson distribution are dpois, ppois, qpois, and rpois. Their definition is similar to those of the binomial distribution (with 1 parameter less). Indeed, every distribution defined in R has functions of the form dxxx, pxxx, qxxx, and rxxx, with xxx the abbreviation of the name of the distribution.

Exercise 3.9 *a. Compute the SD of 1000 samples of a Poisson distribution with $\lambda = 10$. Is the answer as expected?*
b. Plot the cdf's of the Poisson distributions with $\lambda = 1, 5$ and 20 in a single figure.

Exercise 3.10 *A web server can handle 100 requests per minute. Additional demand is lost. Arrivals occur according to Poisson distribution with average 90. Estimate the percentage of requests lost.*
Hint: you can solve this problem by sampling the demand a number of times and calculating for every sample the number of requests lost. You can also obtain the exact result by using the distribution but this is more difficult and less intuitive.

The uniform distribution   The uniform distribution is the first continuous distribution we discuss. It has a minimum and a maximum, commonly denoted with a and b. The defining feature of the uniform distribution is that every interval between a and b of the same length is equally likely. For this reason the cfd, given in Figure 3.4, increases linearly in the interval $[a, b]$ from 0 to 1.

For U uniformly distributed on $[a, b]$, the expectation and standard deviation are as follows:

$$\mathbb{E}U = \frac{a+b}{2} \quad \text{and} \quad \sigma(U) = \frac{b-a}{\sqrt{12}}.$$

The R functions are `dunif`, `punif`, `qunif` and `runif`. E.g., `punif(1,0,3)` gives $1/3$ and `qunif(2/3,0,3)` is equal to 2. See Box 3.6 for the interpretation of `dunif`.

Probabilities of eventualities   Note that `punif(u,a,b)` gives $\mathbb{P}(U \leq u)$ with U uniform with parameters a and b. However, sometimes we are interested in probabilities of other intervals, such as $\mathbb{P}(U > u)$ or $\mathbb{P}(U \in [u,v])$. These expressions can be derived from `punif`. From $\mathbb{P}(U \leq u) + \mathbb{P}(U > u) = 1$ it follows that

$$\mathbb{P}(U > u) = 1 - \mathbb{P}(U \leq u) = 1 - \texttt{punif}(u, a, b).$$

Similarly,

$$\mathbb{P}(U \in [u,v]) = \mathbb{P}(U \leq v) - \mathbb{P}(U \leq u) = \texttt{punif}(v, a, b) - \texttt{punif}(u, a, b).$$

Note that for continuous distributions $\mathbb{P}(X \leq x) = \mathbb{P}(X < x)$. The explanation can be found in Box 3.6. For discrete distributions this does matter!

Intervals like $A = [u, v]$ are called *eventualities*, $\mathbb{P}(A)$ is its probability. As part of the fundamentals of probability more complicated sets A are studied. We will stay far away from this type of mathematical sophistication.

Exercise 3.11 *For U uniformly distributed with parameters 0 and 2, determine by hand $\mathbb{P}(U \in [0.5, 1])$. Check your answer by sampling in R many times from U using* `runif` *and by using* `punif`.

The normal distribution   We continue our focus on distributions with the most famous of them all: the normal or *Gaussian* (after the German scientist) distribution. The normal distribution has two parameters: μ and σ, the expectation and the SD. Be careful: some tools require you to enter the SD, some require the variance. Of course, they are not the same, unless $\sigma = 1$ (or 0, but then there is no variability: the *degenerate distribution* that has as outcome μ with probability 1).

Box 3.6. Probability of a single outcome

A surprising and counter-intuitive feature of continuous distributions is that every possible outcome has probability 0. This is because there are infinitely many points in an interval such as $[a, b]$. If they all had a positive probability of occurring then they would sum up to more than 1. Indeed, if we measure all people in the world up to 10 decimals then nobody would be exactly 1m80. However, we can attribute a probability to intervals, such as all people having a length between 1m80 and 1m81.

For discrete distributions, the R function pxxx gave the probability of a point. For continuous distribution, the definition is different: it gives the so-called *density*. Integrating the density over the real numbers gives 1, just as all probabilities of a discrete distribution sum up to 1.

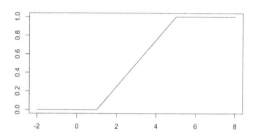

Figure 3.4: The cdf of the uniform distribution with $a = 1$ and $b = 5$

The normal distribution is well-known for its symmetric bell-shaped *density*, which is plotted for two distributions in the left plot of Figure 3.5. The corresponding cdf's (which are easier to interpret) are in the plot on the right. In the figure we used the common notation $N(\mu, \sigma^2)$ for normal distributions. Note the usage of σ^2: thus N(3,4) has SD 2. The N(0,1) is the *standard* normal distribution. The R function for the normal distribution are dnorm, pnorm, etc.

Exercise 3.12 *a. Compute* $\mathbb{P}(X \leq 0)$ *for X standard normal.*
b. Compute $\mathbb{P}(X \geq 1)$ *and* $\mathbb{P}(0 \leq X \leq 1)$.
c. Give the 95th percentile of the standard normal distribution.

Every normal distribution can be derived from the standard normal. If $X \sim N(0,1)$ (meaning that X is N(0,1) distributed), then $Y = \mu + \sigma X \sim N(\mu, \sigma^2)$.

Exercise 3.13 *a. Compute* $\mathbb{P}(X \geq 0)$ *for an* $N(-2, 10)$ *distribution. Do this directly and using the N(0,1) distribution.*

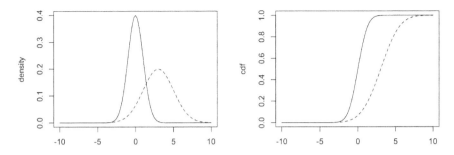

Figure 3.5: Densities and cdf of the normal distributions N(0,1) (solid) and N(3,4) (dashed)

b. Suppose that $x_1, \ldots, x_n$ are samples of a $N(\mu, \sigma^2)$ distribution. How can you turn them into samples of a standard normal distribution?

Let X and Y be independent normally distributed RVs. Because of the formulas on page 39 we have:

$$\mathbb{E}(X+Y) = \mathbb{E}X + \mathbb{E}Y \quad \text{and} \quad \sigma^2(X+Y) = \sigma^2(X) + \sigma^2(Y).$$

Moreover, the normal distribution has a very special property: sums of normal distributions have normal distributions. Note that not all distributions have this property. The normal and binomial distributions (with the same success probabilities) have this property, other distributions such as the uniform have not.

Exercise 3.14 *Sample 10000 times from 2 normally distributed RVs, make a histogram of the sums and convince yourself that the statement above is true. How about $X - Y$? Can you explain this? Do the same thing for two uniform distributions.*

Central limit theorem Earlier, we saw that sums of normal distributions have a normal distribution. But there is more to it: all sums of independent RVs tend to look like normal distributions! For example, if you sum 10 uniform RVs, then the result looks pretty much like a normal distribution. The same holds for averages, as it is just a sum divided by a constant. Recall Equation (3.3) on page 40: $\mathbb{E}\overline{X} = \mathbb{E}X_1$ and $\sigma(\overline{X}) = \sigma(X_1)/\sqrt{n}$. Thus, as n increases, $\overline{X}$ looks more and more like a normal distribution which is more and more concentrated around the mean $\mathbb{E}X_1$. This is called the *central limit* *theorem* (CLT). It is illustrated in Figure 3.6. We see that already the distribution of the average of 10 uniform distributions has the bell shape of the density of a normal distribution.

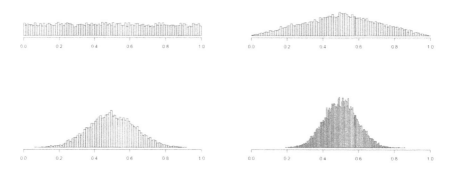

Figure 3.6: Illustration of the CLT: histograms of averages of $1, 2, 5$ and 10 uniform(0,1) realizations

---

Box 3.7. Formal statement of the CLT

The formal statement of the CLT is as follows. First we rescale $\overline{X}$:

$$Z_n = \frac{\sqrt{n}(\overline{X} - \mathbb{E}X_1)}{\sigma}.$$

Now Z_n has $\mathbb{E}Z_n = 0$ and $\sigma^2(Z_n) = 1$. Thus subtracting $\mathbb{E}X_1$ moved the average to 0 and blowing it up with $\sqrt{n}$ avoided it to disappear in 0. The CLT states that Z_n *converges* to a standard normal distribution, i.e., as n increases it looks more and more like a normal distribution which it reaches at ∞.

To make it really formal you have to define convergence of distributions. We won't go into that level of detail.

Averages play an important role in statistics, because we use them as estimators for the expectation (thanks to the LLN). To say something about the accuracy of this estimator, we can use normal distributions (thanks to the CLT). Thus computations with normal distributions are important in statistics. The following rules of thumb are often used, for $X \sim \mathrm{N}(\mu, \sigma^2)$:

- $\mathbb{P}(\mu - \sigma \leq X \leq \mu + \sigma) \approx 68\%$;
- $\mathbb{P}(\mu - 2\sigma \leq X \leq \mu + 2\sigma) \approx 95\%$.

The rule is illustrated in Table 3.7.

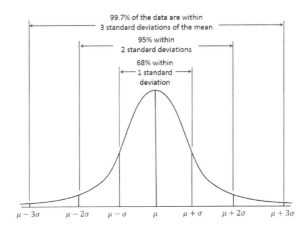

Figure 3.7: Rule of thumb for the normal distribution (source: Wikipedia)

Exercise 3.15 *Reproduce these numbers using* `qnorm` *in R and* `NORM.INV` *in Excel.*

A common error is to apply this rule to all kinds of data and distributions. The answers that you will get are wrong! Sometimes analysts first calculate the average and SD, to use the rule of thumb to find for example the 95th percentile. Not only do they get the wrong answer, there is also a simpler procedure: In a dataset of say 1000 points, they could have taken right away the 950th largest number.

Exercise 3.16 *A hospital performs knee surgery routinely in one of its operating rooms. An operation takes on average 50 minutes with a SD of 20, including cleaning, changing, etc. A session consists of 8 operations, a block of 7 hours is reserved for it. Approximate the probability that the 8 operations take more than the reserved session time. Do this in two ways:*
- use a normal approximation;
- simulate the session many times, assuming that the operations have a uniform distribution.
Note that for the latter exercise you first need to determine the parameters of the uniform distribution.

In the previous exercise, we saw the mathematical theory at work: for theoretical reasons we used a normal distribution, which gave us the same result as the one based on simulation.

The lognormal distribution If data is positive and continuous then they often follow a *lognormal distribution*. Examples are durations of surgery or length of telephone calls. Lognormal RVs are of the form e^X with X a normally distributed RV and e a mathematical constant, e $\approx$ 2.7. A typical density and cdf can be found in Figure 3.8. The distribution is clearly *skewed to the right*. The plots can be made with the following R commands: `curve(dlnorm(x,3,0.5))` and `curve(plnorm(x,3,0.5))`. Note that 3 and 0.5 are the mean and SD at the logscale, of the underlying normal distribution. The real mean and SD are quite complicated formulas of the parameters. Probabilities and quantiles however can easily be derived from the underlying normal distribution. For example, `plnorm(x)` = `pnorm(log(x))`. `LOGNORM.DIST` and `LOGNORM.INV` are the Excel equivalents of `plnorm` and `qlnorm`.

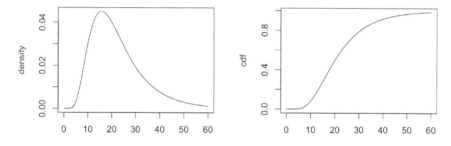

Figure 3.8: Density and cdf of a lognormal distribution

Exercise 3.17 *Find the median of the distribution of Figure 3.8 in 3 ways: using the figure, using* `qlnorm`, *and using* `qnorm`.

Exercise 3.18 *Make a histogram of the product of 2 lognormal distributions. Do you recognize the distribution that you find? What could be the reason? (This requires some mathematical insights.)*

Exercise 3.19 *Sample from a lognormal distribution with mean 10 and SD 5. Note that you first have to compute μ and σ of the underlying normal distribution, the formulas can for example be found on Wikipedia. Check that the sample has indeed the right mean and SD.*

3.4 Parameter estimation

The goal of statistics is to *infer* unknown information from data. For this reason, we sometimes talk of *inferential statistics*, to differentiate from (statistical) data analysis. Data contains noise, for this reason we have to differentiate between noise and signal.

There are basically two ways to proceed. Sometimes you have a hypothesis concerning the experiment that you want to test, for example if a coin is biased. Then we can use *hypothesis testing*. Sometimes we want a reliable estimator of some parameter, such as the average length of a population. This estimator can take the form of an interval, called a *confidence interval*.

Confidence intervals In both hypothesis testing and confidence intervals, the concept of the *sample mean* has a central place, defined in Equation (3.2). Suppose, as an example, we have measured the height of 100 arbitrary adult Dutch men and women and the average is 178 cm. Evidently, the average height of the whole population is not exactly 178 cm, because we took a sample, and we therefore certainly introduced an error. How big is this error? Can we construct an interval in which the true value falls with a certain level of confidence? This confidence interval (CI) is constructed as follows. Suppose that the height of the Dutch follows a distribution X with mean μ and SD σ. Then, according to (3.3) and the CLT, $\overline{X}$ is approximately normal distributed with $\sigma(\overline{X}) = \sigma/\sqrt{n}$. Then a 95% CI is given by $[\overline{X} - 2\sigma/\sqrt{n}, \overline{X} + 2\sigma/\sqrt{n}]$, using the rule of thumb of Figure 3.7. However, we cannot compute this interval: in general we do not know σ. Therefore, we need to estimate it, by the *sample SD*, which is given by

$$S = \sqrt{\frac{\sum_{i=1}^{n}(X_i - \overline{X})^2}{n-1}}.$$

Exercise 3.20 *One would expect n instead of n − 1 in the denominator of S. The reason is that S in its current form is an* unbiased *estimator, i.e.,* $\mathbb{E}S = \sigma$. *Show this. (This exercise requires quite some mathematical skills.)*

In our example, suppose that the sample SD of the height of the Dutch is 5 cm. Then the CI for the average height becomes $[178 - 2 \times 5/\sqrt{100}, 178 + 2 \times 5/\sqrt{100}] = [177, 179]$.

Box 3.8. Interpretation of CI

A CI is commonly interpreted as an interval in which the true value falls with a certain probability. Correctly speaking, this is wrong: μ has an unknown but fixed value so it is within an interval or not. The correct interpretation of a CI is as follows: if you repeat an experiment multiple times and you create a CI every time, then in α (the confidence level) cases μ is inside the interval.

The CI made precise   We said that the 95% CI for the mean is given by $[\overline{X} - 2S/\sqrt{n}, \overline{X} + 2S/\sqrt{n}]$. However, this is not completely true: the 97.5% quantile of the standard normal distribution is 1.96, which can be verified in R with qnorm(0.975).

But there is more to it than that. Because we do not know σ we replaced $(\overline{X} - \mu)/(\sqrt{n}\sigma)$ by $(\overline{X} - \mu)/(\sqrt{n}S)$. While the former has a standard normal distribution, the latter doesn't, because S is a random variable. The true distribution of $(\overline{X} - \mu)/(\sqrt{n}S)$ is called *Student's t-distribution* with $n - 1$ *degrees of freedom*. Thus we should replace 2 by qt(0.975,99), 1.98. We see that the CI gets slightly larger, from 1.96 to 1.98. For larger n, the difference is even smaller, thus in almost all cases 2 is a very good approximation.

Exercise 3.21   *A sample of 200 entries has average 9.8 and sample SD 5.4. Calculate a 90% CI for the population mean.*

Hypothesis testing   In a hypothesis test, we reject a hypothesis when the outcomes are very unlikely when the *null hypothesis* would be true. As an example, assume we want to test whether a coin is unbiased. We throw it 100 times and it comes up heads 62 times. What can we conclude? The standard procedure is to compute the probability of the outcome *or more extreme* under the null hypothesis, which is called the *p-value*. When this p-value is below the *significance level* (often 5%) then we reject the null hypothesis in favor of the *alternative hypothesis*. The probability of 62 or more is 1% (1-pbinom(61,100,0.5)). This is less than 5%, therefore the null hypothesis is rejected: we have sufficient statistical evidence to conclude that the coin is biased.

We actually tested whether heads is more likely to come up then tails. This is called a *one-sided test*. For a *two-sided test* (biased or unbiased, no matter if heads or tails is overrepresented) we have to reserve 2.5% for both sides. Because 1% < 2.5% we still reject. Alternatively, we could multiply the probability by 2. This is actually the standard way to calculate the p-value.

R has a build-in test for this situation: `binom.test`, which should be used as follows: `binom.test(62,100)`. We get as p-value 2% because the default test is 2-sided.

Exercise 3.22 *You roll a die 12 times.*
a. How many sixed do you expect?
b. Assume that no sixes occurred. Can you conclude that the die is biased?

In the exercise, does the p-value mean that we can conclude that the die is *not* biased? The answer is no: if the p-value is higher than 5% no conclusion can be drawn. In this sense, hypothesis testing is asymmetric: only when the p-value is smaller than the significance level can a conclusion be drawn.

When we take a 0/1 sample then we know that the sum is binomial. In general, we do not know the distribution of a sum of RVs and we have to use the CLT. The resulting test for the mean is the *t-test*, again using Student's t-distribution, although a normal approximation is simpler and gives nearly the same results.

As an example, take the average height of adults. Although data is partly unreliable, the average overall world-wide height of adults is around 174 cm. Can we conclude that the Dutch are taller than the worldwide average based on our sample with size 100? Our test is as follows:

$$H_0 : \mu = \mu_0 = 174 \text{ versus } H_1 : \mu > \mu_0 = 174.$$

From `1-pnorm(sqrt(100)*(178-174)/5)` (or, using the mathematically correct t-distribution, `1-pt(sqrt(100)*(178-174)/5,99)` it follows that the p-value is very small. The conclusion is therefore that the null-hypothesis is rejected and that the Dutch are taller than the world average. R also contains commands for directly executing tests. If the data is entered as an array called "data" in R, then you can use `t.test(data,mu=174,alt="g")`, where "g" refers to the alternative hypothesis which is not two-sided, but "greater".

Exercise 3.23 *In this exercise we use the* `beaver1` *dataset in the R* `datasets` *package, which you should install first. Use a t-test to check whether this beaver's average body temperature is significantly different from the average human body temperature (37.3 Celcius). Also determine the p-value directly by computing mean and SD and draw your conclusions.*

Other univariate tests   There are other situations where tests on univariate data (the subject of this chapter) can be very helpful. On the internet, there is ample information on many different tests. Therefore we will not go into all details, we will just give a few of the most often used tests.

Comparing two samples   A frequently occurring task is comparing two datasets to see if their means are equal or not. There are two possibilities: the datasets consists of matched pairs or not. In the case of matched pairs, there is a dependence between the pairs in the two datasets. This is for example the case if you compare incomes between men and women in the same household: you often find high- and low-income couples. A case where the datasets are not matched and perhaps even of different sizes, is when you compare incomes of inhabitants of different cities. To analyse the difference in means we have to determine the difference of the averages. Consider *random samples* X_i and Y_j, with sizes n, and m. As *test statistic T* we take

$$T = \frac{\overline{X} - \overline{Y}}{\sqrt{\frac{S_X^2}{n} + \frac{S_Y^2}{m}}},$$

where S_X and S_Y are the sample SDs. Note that the denominator is equal to $\sigma(\overline{X} - \overline{Y})$ and that T is approximately standard normal, under the null hypothesis. Now we can use the normal distribution to perform our test, or rely on the build-in function of R.

Exercise 3.24 *Now we compare the average body temperatures of* beaver1 *and* beaver2 *in the datasets library. Compute the test statistic and determine whether we reject the null hypothesis that the temperatures are equal. Do this also using the R command* t.test.

Testing for a distribution   Often we are interested to know whether data comes from a certain distribution. However, a test can never confirm that data comes from a certain distribution; it can only tell us how unlikely it is. Different tests consider different aspects of distributions, so it might occur, for exactly the same null hypothesis, but a different statistic, that one test rejects the null hypothesis while another test does not reject.

The Shapiro-Wilk test is a test for normality, with shapiro.test the R command. You do not need to specify the parameters of the normal distribution.

Box 3.9. Q-Q plots

It is a good habit to take a careful look at the data before testing for a distribution. One way to see graphically if a distribution might fit the data is by making a *Q-Q plot*. In a Q-Q plot, we plot the quantiles of the data against those of a certain distribution. A close to straight line indicates that your data might well come from that distribution.

As an example, see the left plot of the figure below, generated by qqnorm(beaver1$temp). In the middle, the line is quite straight; the deviations at the sides indicate outliers. This is confirmed by the histogram on the right. A further confirmation comes from the Shapiro-Wilk test, executed by shapiro.test(beaver1$temp): normality is rejected.

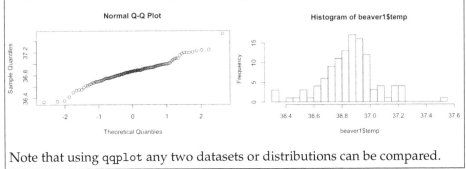

Note that using qqplot any two datasets or distributions can be compared.

Another test is the Kolmogorov-Smirnov test, ks.test in R. It can be used in two ways: to find out if 2 datasets come from the same (continuous) distribution, and to test whether a dataset comes from a given distribution, which has to be specified including its parameters.

Exercise 3.25 *We use the* Nile *dataset in the* datasets *library.*
a. Plot the histogram, boxplot and normal Q-Q plot. Does it look normal?
b. Test for normality.
c. Make a CI for the mean.
d. Split the dataset in two by looking at the first 50 and the last 50 numbers. Is there a significant difference in average?

3.5 Additional reading

There are many books on probability theory. An accessible introduction is Ross [34]. The same holds for statistics. An accessible introduction is Triola [41].

Box 3.10. Bayesian statistics

Central in Bayesian statistics is a distribution on the unknown parameter, such as the mean. This is in contrast with the *frequentist* approach which we discussed so far: there the unknown parameter was unknown but fixed. This distribution on the parameter is updated every time a new observation is made. From the *a priori* distribution we go, using *Bayes' rule*, to the *a posteriori* distribution. This can be done numerically, but for certain distributions analytical results are known.

As an example, consider throwing a possibly biased coin. As initial distribution on the unknown success parameter, we choose the uniform distribution on $[0, 1]$. Every time we throw the coin, we adapt this distribution using Bayes' rule. The resulting distributions are all so-called *beta distributions*. In the figure below we see a number of beta distributions. The top-left figure shows the uniform distribution. After two successes, the posterior distribution is as in the top-right, after 5 successes and 2 failures as in the left-bottom, and after 62 successes and 38 failures as in the right-bottom figure. The equivalent of a CI is a *credible interval*. A 95% credible interval of the last distribution is $[0.52, 0.71]$. This interval was computed with the R commands `qbeta(0.025,63,39)` and `qbeta(0.975,63,39)`.

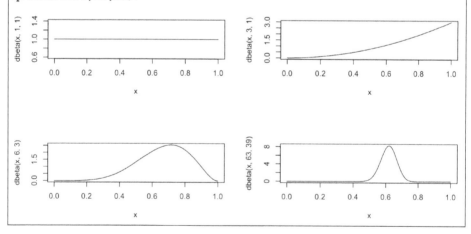

Chapter 4

Machine Learning

In this chapter we focus on models for *multivariate* data. For every entry in the data, we have multiple fields or *attributes*. First we look at *clustering*: can we find groups of data points that are clearly separated from each other? Then we move to models where each entry has a target value that we should explain from the other fields. This target value can be real (any number) or 0/1. In the first case, linear regression (LR) and *deep learning* (a type of *artificial neural network* or ANN) are popular methods. For the 0/1 target we will see how LR and ANN can be adapted to deal with this case. We will also look at *support-vector machines* and *decision trees*. *Forecasting* is a special case of estimation in the situation where one of the fields contains time stamps. We dedicate a separate section to this scenario.

This chapter is entitled *machine learning* (ML), because this name well describes the ideas found within this chapter: using algorithms we discover the values of parameters that describe the structure of the data. This chapter covers the main methods of the field that is nowadays called ML. Note however that ML is a subset of the older field, referred to as *data mining*, and that there is a large overlap with statistics. The difference between ML and statistics has less to do with the methods than with the approach. Statisticians have a more mathematical approach, focusing for example on showing that an algorithm always finds the best parameter values. People with an AI background tend to focus more on computational results. Also, statistics is more focused on small datasets, while typical ML methods need larger datasets (usually a few thousands of observations) to work.

Learning outcomes   On completion of this chapter, you will be able to:

- perform simple machine learning tasks in R

- choose an appropriate method in a given situation

- translate an prediction problem in practice to a machine learning problem

- reflect on the usefulness of machine learning and its pitfalls

4.1   Data preparation

A large proportion of the time devoted to an ML project goes to the preparation of the dataset before the actual ML technique can be executed. In this section we discuss this *data preparation* step. Of course, data preparation is also relevant for univariate data, but because many of the techniques for data preparation concern multivariate data, we discuss it here.

Data preparation consists of the following activities: *data cleansing* (or *cleaning*) and *feature engineering*. *Data wrangling* and *data pre-processing* can be seen as synonyms of data preparation. Especially data wrangling is a more recent term that came into existence with the increase in attention paid to data preparation. Also an additional job title emerged: the *data wrangler*. Another recent job description, with less focus on the algorithms and more on the business side, is *citizen data scientist*.

Regarding data cleansing, data often has missing fields in part of the entries. Many algorithms require all fields to be filled in, often leading to the removal of incomplete records, or to the use of methods such as *mean imputation*, which consists of replacing missing data with the mean of the existing data.

Something else that often occurs are incorrect values, for example negative values for age. Removal or replacement by the average are again possibilities. A better solution however, is to improve the data collection process to avoid missing fields and incorrect values altogether. Indeed, analytics projects lead to more awareness of the importance of data collection and in the end also result in better data. For this reason, in many cases only recent data can be used, sometimes leading to a shortage of data and the risk of *overfitting*, which is the case when a model fits the data well but has no predictive value. This will be discussed in Section 4.4.

Exercise 4.1 *Consider the* `airquality` *data set of the* `datasets` *library. The* `Solar.R` *attribute contains quite a number of missing values indicated with NA* *("not available"). Determine the mean of the non-NA values and replace the NA values by this number.*

Data cleansing requires knowledge of the area of business to which the data relates to be able to understand whether or not data is incorrect. The next step in data preparation—feature engineering—also requires domain knowledge.

Feature engineering consists of different steps. Certain attributes have to be aggregated into appropriate *bins*. For example, the minutes of the day can be aggregated into 24 bins, one for each hour, or even 4: morning, afternoon, evening, night. This is called *binning*. Choices have to be made: do we aggregate income data into "low", "medium" and "high"? Or do we keep the numerical value? This depends on the relation with other attributes, especially the target attribute, and the type of algorithm that will be used.

An important step is the aggregation of multiple attributes into new attributes or *features*, hence the name feature engineering. This often requires inside knowledge of the application area. For example, date and time can be combined into a binary attribute "business hours", when this might be relevant for the problem being studied (e.g., bookings for hotels or flights). Visualisation and insight how attributes correlate are important parts of deciding which attributes to construct and to add. It is not always the case that you first prepare the dataset and then run the ML algorithm once; often you go back and forth between feature selection and learning.

ML methods require structured data as input. For this reason unstructured data such as images and free text have to be transformed into structured data. This requires image recognition and text analytics.

Some methods (such as neural networks) perform better when data is centered and scaled. A standard way to do this is by replacing value x by $(x - \mu)/\sigma$ with μ the average attribute value and σ its standard deviation.

4.2 Clustering

Clustering is the only unsupervised learning technique that we will discuss. Unsupervised learning means there is no target value that we have to approximate or predict. For example, in hotel reservation data we see two separate clusters with different behavior (days of the week, price, time to book), but there is no target attribute with the true value (as in *classification*).

Many different clustering methods exist, depending on the types of data and the objective of the clustering. Here we only describe the most common

---

Box 4.1. Correlation coefficient

The correlation coefficient, or Pearson correlation coefficient, measures the extent to which two variables have a linear relation. It ranges between -1 and 1, with -1 meaning perfect negative correlation, 0 no linear correlation and 1 a perfect positive correlation. Examples with the coefficients are given below.

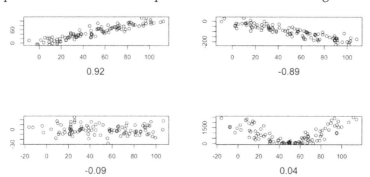

A relation such as in the right-bottom figure suggests a non-linear relation, for example a parabola. In those cases, it is useful to add non-linear attributes, for example x^2, especially when linear regression is used.

Box 4.2. Text mining and image recognition

For unstructured data to be useful in machine learning, features have first to be extracted. This holds true for both images and text. Text mining (today often referred to as *text analytics*) in its simplest form entails looking for keywords in free text fields. More advanced techniques include some form of understanding of text using concepts from linguistics and *information retrieval* (which is the technique behind search engines, which is also about extracting knowledge from free text).

However, these techniques are not always successful in extracting all relevant information out of free text. For this reason, for ML purposes, it is often better to have a limited choice with, for example, a drop-down menu instead of the possibility to enter any text.

Also, image recognition involves the extraction of features from unstructured data, in this case patterns in a 2-dimensional data set with color codes for all pixels. These features are then used as input for ML algorithms, typically *neural networks* with multiple layers (which is called *deep learning* for this reason).

---

one: k-means clustering, used for numerical data. An important property is that the number of clusters found is fixed from the beginning, at say k. We assume we have d numerical attributes, thus every record is a point in the d-dimensional Euclidian space. The algorithm works as follows:

k-MEANS CLUSTERING

initialization	select randomly k points in the d-dimensional Euclidian space
assignment	determine for each record the Euclidian distance to all k points and assign it to the closest
update	move the k points to the *centroid* of each cluster by taking component-wise averages
repeat	repeat the assignment and update steps until the clusters remain the same

See Figure 2.3 on page 25 for an example and for relevant R code.

Exercise 4.2 *Consider the* rock *data set of the* datasets *library. Use k-means to determine 3 clusters and put the centers together with the data in a scatter plot showing* area *and* peri*. Does this correspond to what you expected?*

4.3 Linear regression

Next we study linear regression. This is an important step, because now we move from descriptive methods such as looking at correlations and clustering to predictive methods such as linear regression and neural networks.

In predictive models, there is some *dependent variable* that we want to predict using other variables, the *independent variables*. A dataset with values for the dependent and independent variables is available to *train* or *fit* the model. After that it can be used to predict the dependent variable for points for which we know only the independent variables.

Unfortunately, the outcome is not fully determined by the independent variables: there is also *noise*, which is an unknown component. Therefore, the predictions are never exact. Obviously, it is our goal to get as close as possible.

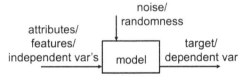

On the other hand, although it may sound counterintuitive, it is sometimes a bad sign when the *fit* is (almost) exact. Certain models have a good fit but they are bad predictors. The reason is that they fit a coincidental pattern in the noise. The same pattern is unlikely to occur for the values to predict, therefore they predict badly. This phenomenon is called *overfitting*.

Box 4.3. Fit versus prediction

The fit is defined as the outcomes of the ML model for the points for which we know the target. The prediction is for points for which we do not know the target value. In the case of temporal data (such as sales per day), we call the prediction the *forecast*. Thus, the fit concerns the past and the forecast the future. (For more on forecasting, see Section 4.5.)

Example 4.1 *Height is strongly correlated to weight of people, therefore height is a good attribute to predict weight. In a particular dataset however, it might be the case that, coincidentally, people born on Wednesday weigh more than those born on other days. Introducing day of the week in our predictive model is an example of overfitting: when we predict the weight of a new group of people, we overestimate for those born on Wednesday, because it is unlikely that they are also heavier. (Although we can never exclude a real correlation: e.g., perhaps the local hospital plans all caesarians for overweight babies on Wednesday.)*

Box 4.4. Overfitting

When the number of variables in a model is not in balance with the number of data points then overfitting can occur. To test for overfitting, it is customary to split the data into a *training set* and a *test set*. Then the model is fit to the training set and it is *validated* on the test set. When this procedure is repeated multiple times on different subsets of the data, then we call this *cross-validation*. This is common practice in ML projects. A rule of thumb is that you should have at least 10 data points per attribute, known as the *one in ten rule*.

In statistics, the terms *in-sample* and *out-of-sample* are used. For example, the in-sample error corresponds to the difference between the model and the actual value on the training set.

A related concept is the *bias-variance trade-off*: when the bias (the difference between signal and fit) is high you miss the signal (*underfitting*); a high variance (of the fit) is an indication of overfitting. While there is a trade-off, a highly predictive model has both a low bias and a low variance.

Linear regression is the most commonly used predictive method.

We approximate or estimate each value $x = (x_1, \ldots, x_d)$ in the d-dimensional attribute space with:

$$\hat{y} = \beta_0 + \beta_1 x_1 + \cdots + \beta_d x_d.$$

The parameters $\beta_0, \ldots, \beta_d$ are determined using a (training) set of known values, with n records, with record i denoted as $(x_{i1}, \ldots, x_{id}, y_i)$. The objective is to get $\hat{y}_i$ and y_i as close as possible in the following way: we minimize the *sum of squared errors* (SSE)

$$\sum_{i=1}^{n} (\hat{y}_i - y_i)^2 = \sum_{i=1}^{n} (\beta_0 + \beta_1 x_{i1} + \cdots + \beta_d x_{id} - y_i)^2.$$

There is an algorithm that finds these βs, called the *least-squares algorithm*. In R you can use it as follows, with the first line omitting all rows with NAs:

```
> aq=na.omit(airquality)
> summary(lm(Ozone~.,data=aq))
```

lm stands for *linear model*, the attribute left of the $\sim$ is the target, "." right of it indicates all other attributes. Let's have a closer look at the output, given below.

```
Residuals:
    Min      1Q  Median      3Q     Max
-37.014 -12.284  -3.302   8.454  95.348

Coefficients:
              Estimate Std. Error t value Pr(>|t|)
(Intercept) -64.11632   23.48249  -2.730  0.00742 **
Solar.R       0.05027    0.02342   2.147  0.03411 *
Wind         -3.31844    0.64451  -5.149 1.23e-06 ***
Temp          1.89579    0.27389   6.922 3.66e-10 ***
Month        -3.03996    1.51346  -2.009  0.04714 *
Day           0.27388    0.22967   1.192  0.23576
---
Signif. codes:  0 '***' 0.001 '**' 0.01 '*' 0.05 '.' 0.1 ' ' 1

Residual standard error: 20.86 on 105 degrees of freedom
Multiple R-squared:  0.6249,    Adjusted R-squared:  0.6071
F-statistic: 34.99 on 5 and 105 DF,  p-value: < 2.2e-16
```

We focus on three values: the estimates of the βs, the p-values of each attribute, and the R^2. From the βs, we see the impact of each attribute on the Ozone level: for example, if the temperature increases by 1 degree, then the Ozone level increases by 1.89. To the right are the p-values. Only Day is above 5% and thus insignificant. Therefore we reduce the model to:

```
> summary(lm(Ozone~Solar.R+Wind+Temp+Month,data=aq))
```

Now Solar.R is not significant, and thus we take:

```
> summary(lm(Ozone~Wind+Temp+Month,data=aq))
```

Now all attributes are significant and we arrive at our final model. This is called the *step-down* approach. Its goal is to separate noise and signal:

statistically speaking it is very unlikely that the dependence on Wind, Temp and Month is due to noise.

Box 4.5. Regularization

Other more general methods to prevent overfitting are known under the name *regularization*. These methods add a penalty term on the regression parameters to the least squares formulation, reducing the number of non-zero parameters and their values. This penalty can be linear (LASSO), quadratic (ridge regression), or a combination of both (elastic net). Applied to the airquality data this leads to models with only Temp, and then, as the weight of the penalty is decreased, Wind, Solar.R and Month are added. The best weight should be determined using cross-validation.

Some R code to get started:
```
> library(glmnet)
> lasso=glmnet(model.matrix(Ozone~.,aq)[,-1],aq[,1],alpha=1)
> predict(lasso,type="coefficients")
```

Therefore, we now have a significant model without overfitting. But is the prediction good? The most common measure compares the SSE with the sum of squared errors of the most naive predictor: the mean. The *coefficient of determination* R^2, which can also be interpreted as the fraction of explained variance, is given by:

$$R^2 = 1 - \frac{\text{SSE of regression}}{\text{SSE of mean}}.$$

R^2 is always between 0 and 1. The closer to 1, the more of the variance is explained by the regression. In the airquality example it is 62%, which is not bad, although 38% of the variability remains unexplained.

The ultimate goal of predictive modeling is to predict the dependent variable for new cases. We predict row 10 of the airquality data set which has NA as Ozone value. The R command:
```
> predict(lm(Ozone~Wind+Temp+Month,data=aq),airquality[10,])
```
gives prediction 36.57.

Exercise 4.3 *Consider the* longley *dataset. Use the step-down method to build a significant model for* Employed. *What is the R squared? Use the model to predict the target for all mean attribute values.*

So far, we discussed LR in its basic form. However, the method is more versatile than the name suggests: the linearity is related to the βs, not to

---

Box 4.6. Causality

Statistical correlation does not necessarily imply *causality*. It regularly happens that there is another hidden variable, called a *confounding variable*, that causes both. Therefore you would need additional evidence to make conclusions concerning causality.

For example, it appears that dog owners are less stressed. This does not necessarily mean that getting a dog will reduce your stress: perhaps people having more time are less stressed and more likely to get a dog. If you give already stressed people the responsibility of a dog, they might even get more stressed... A way to prove that dog ownership reduces stress would be to give dogs to a sufficiently large, randomly selected group of people not owning dogs and study the (long-term) consequences. This is a very costly, if not impossible, thing to do. A more practical approach is to add possible confounding variables to the model. For example, if you add "free time" to the model, the positive effect of dog ownership on stress might disappear.

Box 4.7. Collinearity

In Exercise 4.3 we found a number of independent variables with a very strong linear relation, see below.

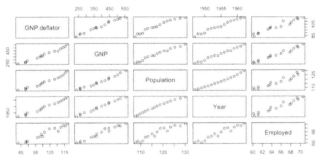

All these variables have approximately the same predictive value (which is also high because of the linear relation with the dependent variable `Employed`). To avoid ambiguity it is better to select one. The choice of variable might also be influenced by causality: it might be better to use `GDP` or `Population` than `Year`. Note that to avoid collinearity it might be interesting to introduce a new variable `GNP per capita`. In the current case the dataset is too small to get significant results.

---

the independent variables. For example, by replacing y~x by y~poly(x,2) you get a quadratic relation (a 2nd-order polynomial).

Exercise 4.4 *Make a data frame with a quadratic function, for example by*
```
> df=data.frame(x=1:20,y=3-(1:20)+0.5*(1:20)^2).
```

Find a perfect fit using `lm`.

Next to adding other functions of a single variable, such as polynomials, we can also introduce functions of multiple variables, such as x_1x_2. These are called *interactions*. You automatically get all interactions if you replace $"+"$ by $"*"$ in the call of `lm`, for example $y \sim x_1 * x_2$ instead of $y \sim x_1 + x_2$.

Exercise 4.5 *Try to improve the results for the* `airquality` *dataset by adding one or more interactions.*

Another important feature are categorical independent variables. If such a variable can take only 2 values, e.g., 0 and 1, then it fits immediately within the framework. But also in the case of multiple values, it is possible to use linear regression, by adding a variable per value. R does this automatically, except when the values are numerical. An example is the `Month` attribute in the `airquality` data frame: it takes values 5–9, which is different from taking May–Sept. When looking at the data, for example by `pairs(airquality)`, we see that the relation between `Month` and `Ozone` is far from linear. This can be solved by making `Month` a *factor*, leading to:

```
> summary(lm(Ozone~Wind+Temp+factor(Month),data=aq))
```

We see that R squared has increased a bit. The method of adding a variable per value for categorical variables is called *one-hot encoding*, the variables are known as *dummy variables*. The statistical theory is known under the name *Analysis of Variation* or ANOVA.

Exercise 4.6 *Analyse the influence of supplement and dose on tooth growth in the dataset* `ToothGrowth`. *Model both variables as categorical. What is the best combination of supplement and dose?*

Box 4.8. Regression towards the mean

The word "regression" in linear regression comes from the concept of *regression towards the mean*: the fact that after an extreme data point the next one is more likely to be close to the mean. "Linear prediction" would probably have been a more accurate term than linear regression.

4.4 Nonlinear prediction

Although linear regression is quite versatile, we are restricted to functions that are linear in the βs. That is, we can model βx, βx^2, and even $\beta x_1 x_2$, but not functions like x^β or $\mathbb{I}\{x \leq \beta\}$ (which is 1 for $x \leq \beta$ and 0 otherwise). Note that, just as in linear regression, x is here the attribute value and β is the parameter of the predictive model. To be able to capture these types of relations we have to consider nonlinear predictive methods, which is the subject of this section. We will discuss *artificial neural networks* and methods originating from *decision trees*.

In LR the output is a linear function of the input, see the formula on page 61 or the figure below. An ANN is a network of nonlinear functions connecting input and output. These functions are of a special form: the output of each node is a nonlinear function such as $\max(0, x)$ with x the weighted sum of the inputs to that node.

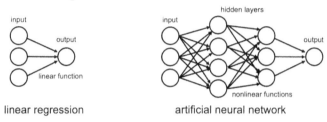

Each arrow in the network has a parameter, and training of the network consists in finding the parameters that minimize the error on the outputs. The algorithm to do this is more complicated and time-consuming than in the case of linear regression, especially when the network has many layers and nodes per layer. This iterative algorithm is called the *backpropagation* algorithm.

Example 4.2 *We will apply the* neuralnet *package to the* airquality *data. An important pre-processing step is to scale all data to numbers between 0 and 1. The R-code is as follows:*

```
> library(neuralnet)
> maxima = apply(aq, 2, max); minima = apply(aq, 2, min)
> aq_scaled = as.data.frame(scale(aq, center = minima,
        scale = maxima - minima))
> nn = neuralnet(Ozone~Solar.R+Wind+Temp+Month,data=aq_scaled,
        hidden=c(5,3))
```

This leads to the following neural net:

As an example of its use, the fit can be calculated as follows:

```
> fit = compute(nn,aq_scaled[,2:5])$net.result*
         (maxima[1]-minima[1])+minima[1]
```

Initial weights are set randomly, therefore the outcomes may differ. The resulting R squared is typically around 85%.

ANNs have many parameters, especially when multiple hidden layers are used. To avoid overfitting, we should always work with a training and a test set, and the net should be trained with as many examples as possible.

Exercise 4.7 *Compute the R squared of the* `airquality` *example. Compare it to the R squared of the linear model. Split the data in a training and a test set, and compute the R squared on the test set using both LR and ANN.*

Exercise 4.8 *Consider the* `iris` *dataset. Use R to train a neural network that predicts* `Sepal.Length` *based on the other attributes. Use it to predict a case of setosa with average* `Sepal.Width`, `Petal.Length` *and* `Petal.Width`.

Box 4.9. Activation functions

The history of ANNs goes back to the 1950s. At the time, there was not sufficient computational power to execute the backpropagation algorithm on sufficiently large networks. Over the last decades, this situation has significantly changed, especially since a new *activation function*, the so-called *ReLU*, is used. Traditionally, the nonlinear function in every node is taken to be the *logistic function* $e^x/(1+e^x)$. This function has many desirable mathematical properties, but an important step in making *deep learning* (ANNs with many hidden layers) work, was the use of the rectified linear unit (ReLU), given by $x^+ = \max(0, x)$.

The use of ANNs with many hidden layers is called *deep learning*. This technique has been very successful in many prediction tasks over the last decades, especially for *image* and *speech recognition*. Deep learning is the technique behind all developments related to autonomous driving. A lot of the technology is publicly available: for example, the R keras library gives an interface to Google's open source library for deep learning *Tensorflow*. Deep learning needs lots of computing power requiring special equipment, such as GPUs (*graphics processing unit*) of which the different cores, used to command different parts of the screen, can now be used to execute back-propagation in parallel. Another aspect of deep learning is that it needs to be configured in the right way, for example by feature engineering. For problems with structured data, a method such as gradient boosting (to be discussed next) works in general better, and it requires little configuration.

Box 4.10. Explainable data science

A big disadvantage of ANNs is that it is hard to understand the model: it is a *black box*, you do not know what is happening inside. In linear regression, the parameters tell us what the impact is of each independent variable, whereas the multitude of parameters in neural nets give us no clue about the impact of each variable. This is a serious drawback of ANNs: decision makers in general want to understand why they need to make a certain decision, not just because the algorithm "says so". There are also situations where black-box predictions lead to ethical questions.

Let us build a *decision tree* for the `airquality` data. The following code prints a tree as text:

```
> library(rpart)
> rpart(Ozone~.,data=aq)
```

A graphical representation of the same tree is given below.

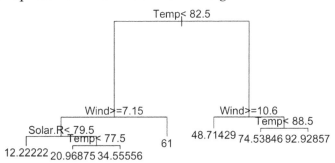

It should be interpreted as follows: for a certain data point, you start at the top, and then, based on the outcomes of the logical statements, you go left for true and right for false until you hit a leaf with a number, which is the prediction for that data point. For example, a day has Temp 80 and Wind 5. Then the prediction is 61: because Temps is smaller than 82.5 you go left, and then right because `Wind>=7.15` is false.

Branches are made on the basis of which logical expression has the highest predictive power, i.e., which one decreases the most the sum of squared errors. This is done iteratively until some stopping criterion is reached.

Exercise 4.9 *Determine the quality of the decision tree for the* airquality *data in the same way as for neural nets.*

Decision trees have several advantages: they are easy to make, also for large data sets, and they are easy to interpret. However, their performance is not very good unless trees with many layers are created, which have the risk of overfitting. There exist extensions, called *ensemble methods*, that use multiple trees and decrease the risk of overfitting. There are two methods: *bagging* and *boosting*.

Bagging is a general method by which multiple, say B predictors are constructed, each using a different training set based on the original one. These B training sets are constructed from the original one by random selection with replacement. For each training set a decision tree is constructed. The final predictor is the average over the B predictors. Compared to a single decision tree, this predictor typically has a lower variance and the same bias. We call this a *bagged tree*. We can further improve the method by selecting the features randomly. This avoids strong correlations between the trees. The resulting set of trees is called a *random forest*.

Exercise 4.10 *Use the* randomForest *R package to create a random forest predictor for the* airquality *data. Determine its performance again using a training and test set.*

It is of interest to note that bagging different methods, i.e., combining different regression methods (such as linear regression and decision trees), works very well in general, because the strong points of the different methods are combined.

Gradient boosting is another ensemble method often used with decision trees. It only assumes you have a prediction method that is just better than taking averages (a so-called *weak learner*). Now you iteratively build up your prediction method: the error of the previous step is (partially) corrected by a new tree. The error of this new set of trees is corrected by yet another tree, etc. The interesting fact is that this procedure (called a *meta-algorithm* because it uses other algorithms as input) produces a *strong learner*: a prediction that reaches an arbitrary precision when applied to enough data.

Gradient boosted decision trees is one of the most popular and most successful ML methods today, winning many recent Kaggle competitions. Because it is based on trees, it gives (some) insight into the importance of attributes and it works well "out-of-the-box".

Exercise 4.11 *Use the* xgboost *R package to create a gradient boosting predictor for the* airquality *data. Determine its performance again using a training and test set.*

Exercise 4.12 *Consider the* iris *dataset. Use R to train a decision tree, a random forest and gradient boosting to predict* Sepal.Length *based on the other attributes. Use it to predict a case of* setosa *with average* Sepal.Width, Petal.Length *and* Petal.Width.

4.5 Forecasting

Forecasting is a special kind of prediction involving temporal data, i.e., data which is ordered by time. Examples are quarterly unemployment rates, daily sales of a product and heart-rate measurements made every second by a fitness tracker. In the scientific literature there is a strong bias towards long-term economic data, but today most of the data is automatically collected *high-frequency data*. Because it is a special case of prediction, the methods discussed in the previous section can sometimes be applied successfully. However, *time series* (data with time stamps) often have special features that make dedicated forecasting methods work better. Indeed, we often see seasonality (for example, the same patterns occuring every year), errors on consecutive days that depend on each other (violating standard assumptions), and the fact that older data is often less relevant. Over the last century many special-purpose algorithms have been developed, mainly by statisticians and econometrists. The most important ones are smoothing methods and ARIMA (see Box 4.12). Our focus will be on the highly successful smoothing methods.

Time series usually consist of three components: trend, seasonality, and noise. Trend is the long-term level. Seasonality concerns fixed-length cycles, usually of a year, week or day. Noise is random short-term fluctuations.

Box 4.11. M-competitions

Many different forecasting methods exist, but which one is best? A number of competitions have been organized by the forecasting specialist S. Makridakis, and therefore called the *M-competitions*. The most recent one at the writing of this book (M4) took place in the first half of 2018. A number of conclusions can be drawn:
- mathematical sophistication is not a guarantee for better forecasts;
- pure ML methods such as deep learning are less good than traditional statistical methods;
- combining (*bagging*) methods improves the forecasting accuracy.

Box 4.12. ARIMA

ARIMA stand for *auto-regressive integrative moving-average*, and is a mathematical model where the error and the parameters depend on previous errors and parameters. A mathematically beautiful theory, but a black box that usually performs worse than methods based on decomposition or smoothing. For this reason it is seldomly applied in practice.

Example 4.3 *Sales data show all three components. Sales might increase or decrease over time depending on market share, competition, economic situation, etc. This is part of the trend. Sales of consumer articles often show a strong end-of-year peak: this is intra-year seasonality. Sales also depend on the day of the week and the hour of the day, which is the intra-week and intra-day seasonality. Finally, even the best forecasting algorithm cannot forecast with 100% accuracy: what remains is noise.*

An obvious way to forecast is to take time and seasonality (using one-hot encoding) as independent variables and use one of the methods of the previous sections.

Example 4.4 *The* `AirPassengers` *data set contains 12 years of monthly data. By adding a variable with the names of the months, we model trend and seasonality at the same time. With the following code we can make a linear model, with a 2-year forecast as shown in the left plot:*

```
> time=1:144; months=rep(month.abb,12)
> fit=lm(AirPassengers~time+months)
> fc=predict(fit,data.frame(time=145:168,months=month.abb))
```

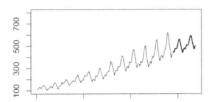 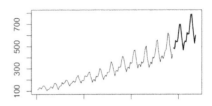

The seasonality of the forecast is not big enough: it does not scale with the trend, which is what we could have expected from a linear model. By transforming the data first (by taking logarithms) and then later taking exponentials, of the forecast we get the better forecast on the right-hand side.

As the objective used in forecasting we usually take the *root mean squared error* (RMSE).

Exercise 4.13 *Repeat both forecasting methods from the example above but now with a training set of 10 years and the last two years as test set. Compute the RMSE for both methods.*

Disadvantages of using a standard prediction method such as linear regression are that trend changes are easily missed and that recent data has the same influence on the forecast as older data. For these reasons dedicated methods such as smoothing work better.

Smoothing in its simplest form works as follows. Suppose we have data without seasonality nor trend. Then two naive forecasts are: take the average of all data or just the last data point. The average filters out the noise in the best way, but uses data that is too old. Taking one data point has the disadvantage that it projects today's variability on the future. Smoothing is the perfect middle ground: it gives exponentially decreasing weights to the past. Let $y_1, \ldots, y_t$ be the observations up until now, time t. Then the forecast at t, $\hat{y}_t$, is given by:

$$\hat{y}_t = \alpha y_t + \alpha(1-\alpha)y_{t-1} + \alpha(1-\alpha)^2 y_{t-2} + \cdots,$$

with $\alpha \in (0,1)$ some parameter. The nice thing about this form of smoothing (called *simple exponential smoothing* or SES) is that it gives a simple recursion:

$$\hat{y}_t = \alpha y_t + (1-\alpha)\hat{y}_{t-1}. \tag{4.1}$$

This was especially handy in the days that computations still had to be done by hand.

SES can be extended to allow for slope, just as LR. This requires a slope forecast with a second smoothing parameter, usually called β. This method is known as *Holt's method*. When we also include smoothed seasonality factors then we get the *Holt-Winters method*. It is part of the `forecast` package and can be called with `hw()`.

Exercise 4.14 *Apply Holt-Winters to the* `AirPassenger` *data and compute the RMSE in the same way as in Exercise 4.13.*

A method that we have not discussed yet is *decomposition*. Decomposition in its simplest form filters out the seasonality by taking *moving averages* of the length of the seasonal cycle. Then the remaining trend is estimated by, for example, linear regression. The average difference between trend and actual is the seasonal component. As an example, the R `prophet` forecasting library developed by Facebook Research for high-frequency data is based on decomposition. The `forecast` R library also has decomposition functionality. For the logs of the `AirPassenger` data we can use the command `plot(decompose(log(AirPassengers)))` leading to:

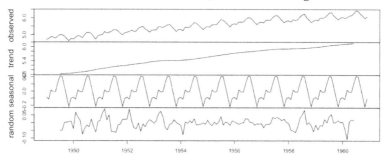

We see the original (log-transformed) data, the trend, the seasonal pattern, and the remaining errors.

Exercise 4.15 *In this exercise we use the* `UKgas` *dataset. Apply the Holt-Winters method for different smoothing parameters. Apply ARIMA with a seasonal component using the* `auto.arima()` *function. Compare both methods using a plot and by computing the RMSEs on a well-chosen test set.*

4.6   Classification

Up to now we considered numerical-valued target variables, which is generally called regression. In this section, we consider categorical target vari-

---

Box 4.13. Explanatory variables

Sometimes other variables offer additional information. They are called explanatory variables. In models based on linear regression they are easy to add. The ARIMA framework can be extended to ARIMAX to include these variables.

---

ables. This is called *classification*. We focus on the case of two classes; some methods can easily be extended to more than two. One by one we discuss how to extend the regression methods to classification.

Note that if we have two categories, classification amounts to selecting 0 or 1. Linear regression can be extended to classification by adding a function that maps the dependent variable to $[0, 1]$. The outcome is to be interpreted as the likelihood of 0 or 1, and a fit or prediction can be obtained by rounding. The function which is used is the *logistic function* $e^x / (1 + e^x)$ (see below). For this reason this technique is called *logistic regression*.

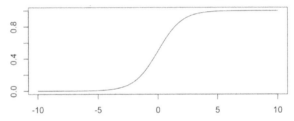

After rounding to 0 or 1 the counts of the possible outcomes of the fit and the actuals can be tabulated in a 2×2 *confusion matrix*.

Example 4.5 *We use the* PimaIndiansDiabetes *data from the* mlbench *library. We predict* diabetes *from the other attributes by*

```
> fit=glm(diabetes~.,data=PimaIndiansDiabetes,family=binomial)
> predict(fit,type="response")>0.5
```

Here glm *stands for* generalized linear model, *and* family=binomial *assures we are doing logistic regression. The predictions can by used together with a* table() *command to produce the confusion matrix:*

```
                 actuals
    predictions pos neg
            pos 156  55
            neg 112 445
```

As an example, 112 people having diabetes were not classified as diabetic, so-called "false negatives". From the confusion matrix many different measures can

be derived, such as the fraction of rightly classified people, called the accuracy:
$(156 + 445)/(156 + 55 + 112 + 445) = 78\%$.

Exercise 4.16 *Look up the definitions of sensitivity, specificity and precision (for example, at the Wikipedia entry of "confusion matrix") and compute them for the example above.*
Compute sensitivity and specificity for different values of the cut-off point (which was 0.5) and put them both in a plot with the cut-off point ranging from 0 to 1.

Deciding which measure to choose is not always easy. However, we should keep in mind that classification usually is not a goal by itself, but is used to make decisions. For example, regulations might require that the sensitivity is at least 95%, or it may be the case that false negatives are more expensive than false positives. This might help us determine the measure to use.

Exercise 4.17 *Suppose in the example that false negatives are 10 times more expensive than false positives. What is the optimal cut-off point and what are the costs?*

Box 4.14. Unbalanced datasets

In the diabetes data 35% is positive. Therefore it is easy to obtain an accuracy of 65%: simply classify everybody as negative. This is an example of unbalanced data, and many datasets are even more unbalanced. Different methods exist to counter the averse consequences of unbalanced datasets, depending also on the technique used. They include changing the objective of the ML algorithm, and deleting or duplicating data to make the dataset balanced.

The `neuralnet` function can also be used to do classification with ANNs. To indicate the logistic activation function we use the following additional arguments: `act.fct="logistic"`, `linear.output=FALSE`. The confusion matrix is as follows:

```
                actuals
predictions pos neg
        pos 190  77
        neg  78 423
```

As can be seen, the precision is a bit higher than for logistic regression. We used 2 hidden layers which contain each 2 nodes.

Exercise 4.18 *For the* `PimaIndiansDiabetes` *dataset, run logistic regression and a neural net for training and test sets of 70 and 30% of the data. Which method do you prefer and why?*

It is very natural to use decision trees for classification. The command `rpart(diabetes~.,data=PimaIndiansDiabetes)` gives the decision tree of Figure 4.1.

Figure 4.1: A decision tree for classification

Exercise 4.19 *Determine the confusion matrix for the decision tree using the training and test set of Exercise 4.18.*

Random forests and gradient boosting can also be used for classification. We finish this section on classification with a technique that is specially designed for classification: *support-vector machines*. It creates the hyperplane (an $(n-1)$-dimensional plane in the n-dimensional feature space) that best separates the categories.

Calling `svm(diabetes~.,data=PimaIndiansDiabetes)` from the e1071 R package (named after a Vienna computer science department), leads to the following confusion matrix:

```
                actuals
predictions pos neg
        pos 170  37
        neg  98 463
```

Exercise 4.20 *Determine the confusion matrix for the support-vector machine using the training and test sets of Exercise 4.18.*

4.7   Additional reading

Kaggle.com is an online platform for ML challenges where some of the world's best specialists compete for the prize money. Note that Netflix played an important role in popularizing competitions: the so-called *Netflix competition* consisted of building a recommender system for movies in the time that Netflix was still a relatively unknown company.

Good books on predictive modeling that are not overly technical are Kuhn & Johnson [23] and Hastie et al, [16]. Géron [12] also includes many details on how to get advanced neural networks working using TensorFlow, distributed computing, etc. The website www.3blue1brown.com contains some great videos on neural networks. Manning et al. [25] is a text book on information retrieval.

A good starting point for text mining in R is Silge & Robinson [38], which is also available online.

A practical and accessible text on forecasting is Hyndman & Athanasopoulos [18], which can also be read online. It makes extensive use of the R forecast library. More details on the M4 competition can be found in Makridakis et al. [24].

Chapter 5

Simulation

Simulation can be used in cases where we know exactly how the attributes or *components* of some *system* interact to give a dependent value or output. Therefore simulation is a purely predictive method by which we can model any form of dependency. However, contrary to machine-learning models, the input is random. Simulation determines the random impact of the input on the output. For example, we can quantify the impact on waiting times of having an additional cashier in a supermarket or an additional lane in a road network. In these examples, the randomness comes from the unknown behavior of the customers or drivers.

Learning outcomes   On completion of this chapter, you will be able to:

- describe Monte Carlo and discrete-event simulation

- perform Monte Carlo simulations in R and Excel

- translate business simulation problems into simulation models

- reflect on the usefulness of simulation in practice

5.1   Monte Carlo simulation

Suppose there are k inputs and some known function g that relates the inputs to the output, i.e., for inputs $x_1, \ldots, x_k$ the output is $y = g(x_1, \ldots, x_k)$. The central question in simulation is: can we give a reliable estimate of the expected output $\mathbb{E}Y = \mathbb{E}g(X_1, \ldots, X_k)$? We assume that $X_1, \ldots, X_k$ are know random variables which we often assume to be independent. We estimate $\mathbb{E}Y$ by repeatedly sampling from $(X_1, \ldots, X_k)$ and computing g. Let us call the outcomes $Y_1, \ldots, Y_n)$. Then, according to the law of large numbers (see page 40), the average $\overline{Y}$ is an estimator for $\mathbb{E}Y$.

Example 5.1 *A* project *consists of a number of activities with precedence constraints: an activity can only be started when all the preceding ones are finished. For example, the roof of a house can only be constructed when the walls are finished. Clearly,* project planning *is an important part of* project management. *The essence of projects is that each project is different. Therefore we cannot predict activity durations with certainty (as we can in manufacturing, for example following the* lean *approach). As a simple example, suppose we have two parallel activities followed by a third activity. Then the duration of the project is* $g(x_1, x_2, x_3) = \max\{x_1, x_2\} + x_3$. *Assume all three durations have uniform* $[0, 2]$ *distributions (which have mean equal to 1). Then we can approximate the expected duration of the project with the following R command:*

```
> mean(pmax(runif(n,0,2),runif(n,0,2))+runif(n,0,2))
```

with n equal to say 10000. With seed 0 this gives 2.33 as answer.

    Note that this is substantially more than 2, which would have been the answer in the case of deterministic durations with the same mean. Mistaking the duration of the means for the mean of the durations is a common mistake, called the strong form of the flaw of averages *by Savage [36].*

It is logical to question the accuracy of the answer. In simulation it is common to construct a confidence interval for the outcome. As shown on page 49, a 95% CI is given by $[m - 2s/\sqrt{n}, m + 2s/\sqrt{n}]$, with m the average outcome and s its SD.

Example 5.2 *Based on the same durations we can compute the sample SD of the small example project: 0.75. The CI is* $[2.31, 2.34]$.

Note that, as long as the simulations are relatively simple, we can take the sample size n as big as we like and thereby obtain an arbitrarily accurate answer.

Exercise 5.1 *a. Explain the difference between the R functions* max *and* pmax.
b. Using R, simulate the project of Figure 6.5 on page 92, with all activities having uniform distributions with mean as indicated and width $(b - a)$ *equal to 2. Compute a CI.*

Box 5.1. Simulation in Excel

Microsoft Excel or comparable spreadsheets are less appropriate for simulation. By using F9 the sheet is recalculated, and all random variables are sampled again. However, this does not allow us to compute a CI. This can be done by putting the whole simulation on 1 row and copying that row many times. Add-ins to Excel exist (such as Crystal Ball) that add simulation functionality to Excel.

---

c. Simulate the project again with all activities having lognormal distributions with mean as indicated and SD 1. Note that the mean and SD of the underlying normal distributions first need to be computed (see also Exercise 3.19).

Exercise 5.2 *Repeat parts b) and c) of the previous exercise using Excel.*

Box 5.2. Tail probabilities

Sometimes we are not interested in the expectation of $g(X_1,,\ldots,X_k)$, but in probabilities of the form $\mathbb{P}(g(X_1,,\ldots,X_k) \geq \alpha)$. However, a probability can be written as an expectation:

$$\mathbb{P}(g(X) \geq \alpha) = \sum_{g(x) \geq \alpha} \mathbb{P}(X = x) = \sum \mathbb{I}\{g(x) \geq \alpha\}\mathbb{P}(X = x) = \mathbb{E}\mathbb{I}(g(X) \geq \alpha),$$

with $\mathbb{I}$ a special function, which is 1 when the argument is true and 0 otherwise, called the *indicator* function. Thus we end up estimating the expectation of the 0/1 function $\mathbb{I}(g(X) \geq \alpha)$. For example, in the project planning example we are interested in the fraction of times that the project takes more than 2 time units. In R we compute this as follows:

```
> durations=pmax(runif(n,0,2),runif(n,0,2))+runif(n,0,2)
> m=mean(durations>2);s=sd(durations>2)
> c(m-2*s/sqrt(n),m+2*s/sqrt(n))
```

This gives as CI $[0.65, 0.67]$.

Exercise 5.3 *The budget of most companies are set without taking the variability of the numbers into account. Consider a simple budget:*

$$profit = sales \times (price - variable\ costs) - fixed\ costs.$$

All components depend on market situations and are random; for simplicity we assume them to be independent. They can be assumed to have normal distributions, with mean and SD 10000 and 1000 for sales, 100 and 20 for the price, 80 and 10

for the variable costs, and 100000 and 20000 for the fixed costs.
a. Simulate the expected profit and determine a CI.
b. Could you have calculated the answer without simulation? Explain your answer.
c. Determine the probability of a loss and a CI of this probability. Hint: first read Box 5.2 on "tail probabilities".

Box 5.3. Machine learning versus simulation

Most machine-learning methods consist of two phases: first a descriptive phase in which a model is learned, within a certain class of models, such as linear with normally distributed noise. The second phase is the predictive part in which the output for new, deterministic, inputs is approximated. Simulation only consists of a predictive part, without restrictions on the model. It quantifies the consequences of uncertainty on the input to the output. Simulation can also be used for the predictive phase of a machine-learning model in case the input is random.

5.2 Discrete-event simulation

Sometimes a system is too complex to be modeled by some function g. This is especially the case when it concerns a process that evolves randomly over time. In such a situation *discrete-event simulation* (DES) is required. A central concept in DES is the *state*, which changes at random points in time. The state is discrete in nature, hence the name. The output or performance is usually a function of the state, averaged over time. The simulation is often terminated after a fixed amount of time, or when some condition is satisfied. We are usually interested in the expectation of the output measure. As the output of every run is a random variable, we can calculate a CI in the same way as we did for the Monte Carlo simulation.

Example 5.3 *The evolution of waiting queues in a service center or the inventory positions in a warehouse are typical examples of processes that can be modeled using DES. Examples in other areas are the evolution of a disease in a body or the state of a communication network.*

In these examples, the state refers to the number of customers in the service center, the stock in the warehouse, the extent to which the disease has progressed, or the numbers of data packets *in each buffer in the network routers, respectively.*

In the service center we might be interested in the average waiting time during a day. In the warehouse we might be interested in the long-run probability of having no stock. In the case of the progression of a disease we might be interested in the time until death, while in the network situation we might be interested in the percentage of packets lost due to buffer overflow.

When employing DES there are two very distinct options: you can program the simulation in a programming language, or you can use a (graphical) tool. For certain programming languages there are libraries available with useful entities for simulation, but most code has to be programmed. Graphical simulation tools require less programming. For an impression of how such a tool works see, Figure 5.1. You can drag and drop components at the left to make a model in the middle. By clicking on the components they can be configured. A large number of graphical simulation tools exist, mostly proprietary, some of them focused on specific applications. The advantages of both methods are clear: programming offers flexibility and computational speed; using a tool offers speed in implementation plus a configurable graphical interface to impress customers.

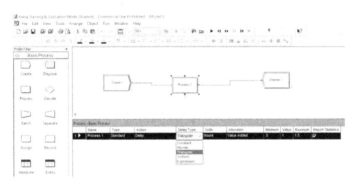

Figure 5.1: An impression of a simple model in the Arena DES tool

---

Box 5.4. Object-oriented programming
Simulation lends itself perfectly to object-oriented (OO) programming, which is the paradigm behind many modern programming languages such as Java, C++ and C#. In fact, the simulation language Simula, developed in the 1960s, is generally considered to be the first OO programming language. It had a considerable influence on current-day OO languages.

Exercise 5.4 *Consider a small intensive care units with 2 beds. Patients arrive with exponentially distributed interarrival times, on average every 8 hours. Patients stay for a lognormal duration with parameters 1 and 1. When both beds are*

occupied patients are transferred to a different hospital. Simulate this ICU for one week and count the number of transfers. Do this for multiple runs and construct a CI.

This exercise requires programming experience. It is useful to store and update at the time of each event the current time, the number of occupied beds, and times of the next arrival and departures. There is a Wikipedia page with details of the exponential distribution.

Validation   Statistics and ML also play an important role in DES, but in a different way than when you apply them directly. In simulation the system under study is considered to be composed of components, who interact in a known way. However, to derive the parameters of the components and their interaction we need statistics and ML. *Validation* is concerned with the question to which extend the simulation reflects reality, i.e., to which extent errors in the components and their interaction propagate to the level of the performance measures. Therefore, the parameters of the components are determined using appropriate ML techniques, and then the performance of the simulation is compared to that of the real system. An accurate approximation of the components does not guarantee an accurate output: (simulation) models can be more or less *robust* to parameter errors.

Validation is rarely easy, often because of a lack of data. Quite often the differences between reality and simulation are so big that statistical tests for equality are always rejected. This does not mean that simulation is useless. In evaluating the differences, we should always take the goal of the simulation into account. Still, in many situations simulations can only be validated after considerable effort or even tuning (where certain parameters are adapted to make the simulation model fit reality). Simulation should only be used after careful consideration: implementing simulation is time-consuming and there is no guarantee of reliable results.

Example 5.4 *Consider an emergency department (ED) of a hospital. Every ED has limited care facilities, often leading to congestion and delays. Four hours is generally considered to be the limit to the length of stay of patients at an ED. Our ED wants to analyze the factors that lead to higher numbers of patients staying longer than 4 hours.*

Simulation requires many resources within the ED to be modeled: triage nurses, doctors with different specialties, beds, radiology equipment, etc. For all these resources, parameters such as their duration have to be determined, as well as the routing between the resources, priority of treatment, etc. Reliable data is hard to get, among other reasons because data entry is of little importance and because of the omnipresence of ad-hoc decisions. This lack of reliable data often translates into output that is far from reality. This makes simulation of limited use to systems where human decision making plays such a central role.

We could use an ML approach directly. We should engineer our features as to obtain parameters of interest. Then we could train our model and determine the impact of, for example, high numbers of arrivals or lateness of doctors on the length of stay at the ED. There is no such thing as validation in ML; the risk here is overfitting.

An ML approach is much faster than simulation and often gives very good results. In certain situations, we cannot avoid the use of simulations, especially when we are interested in situations where we do not have data. For example, suppose we want to change the routing in the ED. Then all components are analyzed using historical data. The model is validated on the current way of working, and then the new situation is simulated.

Box 5.5. Long-run performance

Sometimes there is no natural termination moment for the simulation. In the supermarket example a day might be the right time frame, but in the network simulation there might not be such a moment. We are interested in the long-run *stationary* performance for constant parameters. Under certain conditions it can be shown (using the LLN) mathematically that the long-run average performance approaches the long-run expected performance. Because we cannot simulate for an infinitely long period, and because a single run does not give us information on the variability, it is customary to take the average over a number of runs. To avoid different "start-up" behavior, the first part of each simulation is not counted. See the figure below for an illustration of a service center with 10 counters. We clearly see the average over 100 runs increasing from the empty initial situation to around 15, and two runs constantly fluctuating.

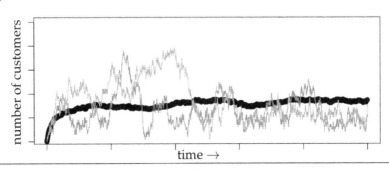

5.3   Additional reading

There are many books on the mathematical aspects of simulation. See, e.g., Ross [33]. Kelton et al. [20] is an example of a book which is more focused on modeling and tooling (especially the discrete-event simulation tool Arena). There is a list of discrete-event software tools on Wikipedia.

Savage [36] uses simulation to explain variability and its pitfalls to layman, avoiding words such as *random variable*. Klastorin [21] is an excellent book on project management.

More information on the OO simulation language Simula can be found on Wikipedia.

Chapter 6

Linear Optimization

In this chapter we discuss linear optimization problems. It is a framework used successfully in many industries to solve a broad variety of problems. We discuss different types of linear problems and show how you can solve them in Excel and R.

Learning outcomes   On completion of this chapter, you will be able to:

- implement linear optimization problems in R, Excel and dedicated modeling languages

- model appropriate business problems as linear optimization models

- reflect on the usefulness and applicability of linear optimization

6.1   Problem formulation

We introduce linear optimization through an example. Later on we will give the general formulation.

Assume a company has n products which it can produce using m resources of which there is only a limited amount available. The problem to solve is which quantities to produce of each product such that the revenue is maximized and the resource constraints are satisfied. Examples of this *product-mix problem* are refineries combining different types of crude oil into end products, a farmer dividing his land between crops with constraints on the amount of fertilizer or environmental impact, etc.

85

Let us consider a simple *instance* of this problem. A company has 2 differents products, for example 2 types of crops, with profit 2 and 3 per quantity produced. We also have 2 resources: fertilizer and land. Product 1 requires 1 unit (e.g., ton) of fertilizer and 1 unit (e.g., acre) of land per unit produced, product 2 requires only 2 units of land. The availability of the resources is as follows: 5 units of fertilizer, 10 units of land. What is the optimal product mix?

This problem has a structure in which we can apply to many optimization problems:
- there are *decision variables* that have to be chosen;
- there is an *objective* that needs to be maximized;
- there are *constraints* which need to be satisfied.

In mathematical terms, our instance becomes:

maximize $2x_1 + 3x_2$ (objective)

subject to

$x_1 \leq 5$ (constraint resource 1)
$x_1 + 2x_2 \leq 10$ (constraint resource 2)
$x_1, x_2 \geq 0.$

Because the functions $2x_1 + 3x_2$, x_1 and $x_1 + 2x_2$ are linear in $x = (x_1, x_2)$ we call this a *linear optimization* (LO) problem. For LO, efficient *solvers* exist that are guaranteed to give an optimal solution, even for problems with thousands of variables and constraints. To solve our instance with R, the following code can be used:

```
> install.packages("lpSolve")   (install solver package (use only once))
> library(lpSolve)                               (load library)
> f.obj <- c(2, 3)                               (set objective)
> f.con <- matrix (c(1, 0, 1, 2), nrow=2, byrow=TRUE)
                                                 (constraint values)
> f.dir <- c("<=", "<=")                         (constraint types)
> f.rhs <- c(5, 10)                              (resource amounts)
> lp ("max", f.obj, f.con, f.dir, f.rhs)         (get optimal value)
> lp ("max", f.obj, f.con, f.dir, f.rhs)$solution
                                                 (get optimal solution)
```

Exercise 6.1 *Solve the problem of Section 6.2 with R.*

There are different ways to understand what the R solver did. Let us first take a graphical look. In Figure 6.1 the problem is drawn with x_1 on the horizontal axis and x_2 on the vertical one. We see the two constraints who together with the non-negativity constraints ($x_1, x_2 \geq 0$, assumed by default) delimit the allowable area, often called the *feasible region*. Because of the linearity of the constraints and the objective, the optimum (if it exists, see below) must be at the edge, at a corner. To determine the optimal corner, we slide a line with equal objective value until we hit the feasible region, i.e., the set of points that satisfy all constraints. The line with value 36 is drawn in the figure. When we slide it down it hits the feasible region in the point with $x_1 = 5$ and $x_1 + 2x_2 = 10$. From this, the optimal solution follows again: $x_1 = 5$ and $x_2 = 2.5$.

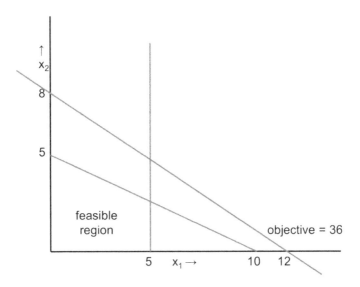

Figure 6.1: A graphical view of LO

Let us now take an algebraic point of view. The 2 constraints can be rewritten as equalities as follows, using additional variables y_1 and y_2:

$$
\begin{array}{lcl}
x_1 \leq 5 & & x_1 + y_1 = 5 \\
x_1 + 2x_2 \leq 10 & \Leftrightarrow & x_1 + 2x_2 + y_2 = 10 \\
x_1, x_2 \geq 0 & & x_1, x_2, y_1, y_2 \geq 0
\end{array}
$$

We have 2 equalities and 4 variables. This means that 2 non-zero variables suffice to find a solution. All 4 corners of the feasible region correspond to such a solution. The interior corresponds to solutions for which all variables are positive. The corners correspond to the following solutions:

- $(x_1, x_2, y_1, y_2) = (0, 0, 5, 10)$, origin;
- $(x_1, x_2, y_1, y_2) = (0, 5, 5, 0)$, upper-left corner;
- $(x_1, x_2, y_1, y_2) = (5, 0, 0, 5)$, lower-right corner;
- $(x_1, x_2, y_1, y_2) = (5, 2.5, 0, 0)$, upper-right corner (the optimum).

The algorithm implemented in the solver hops from corner to corner until it cannot improve the objective value anymore. This method is called the *simplex algorithm*.

Box 6.1. History of Linear Optimization

Several researchers have formulated Linear Optimization problems but it was G.B. Dantzig (1914-2005) who invented in 1947 the simplex algorithm. Dantzig was an American scientist with German-French roots. At the time, until very recently, it was commonly known as linear *programming*. LO has been extremely useful for solving all kinds of business problems and is by far the most successful technique within operations research.

Its random, dynamic counterpart is called *dynamic programming* (see Chapter 9), developed by R.E. Bellman (1920-1984). This division between deterministic and random problems is still very visible in operations research theory and applications.

The general formulation of an LO problem is as follows, for n decision variables and m constraints:

$$\text{maximize} \sum_{i=1}^{n} p_i x_i \qquad \text{(objective)}$$

subject to

$$\sum_{j=1}^{n} a_{ij} x_j \leq b_i, i = 1, \ldots, m \qquad \text{(constraints)}$$

$$x_1, \ldots, x_n \geq 0.$$

Instances where the objective needs to be minimized or with constraints of the form "$=$" or "$\geq$" can be rewritten to fit the general formulation.

Exercise 6.2 *Consider the following LO problem:*

$$\text{minimize } 2x_1 + x_2 + 4x_3 \qquad \text{(objective)}$$

subject to

$$x_1 - 2x_2 + 2x_3 \leq 120$$
$$-x_1 - x_2 + 3x_3 = 100$$
$$x_1 - x_2 + x_3 \geq 80$$
$$x_i \geq 0 \text{ for all } i.$$

a. Solve it in R (see the online documentation of the R package lpSolve *to find out how to change the signs of the constraints).*

b. Rewrite it in the general form with maximization and "≤" constraints.
c. Solve this problem in R.

Sometimes we write the general formulation in matrix notation. Then it becomes:

$$\max\{p^T x \mid Ax \le b, x \ge 0\},$$

where p and x are n-dimensional column vectors (and thus p transposed, p^T, is a row vector), b is an m-dimensional column vector, and A is an $m \times n$ matrix.

Not all LO problems can be solved. Sometimes the problem is unbounded, meaning that solutions of arbitrarily large values can be found. On the other hand, there are also problems where there are no feasible solutions at all. In Figure 6.2 examples of both situations are shown.

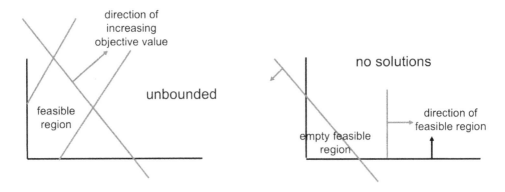

Figure 6.2: An unbounded (left) and an infeasible (right) LO problem

Exercise 6.3 *Enter both problems of Figure 6.2 in R and see what output you get.*

6.2 LO in Excel

To solve LO problems in Excel, you should first make sure that the "solver add-in" is installed. You can check its availability under "Tools". How to install it depends on your version of Excel, for more details do a Google search for "install Excel solver".

Now we show how to solve the following problem using Excel:

$$\text{maximize } 2x_1 + 4x_2 + 8x_3 \qquad \text{(objective)}$$

subject to

$$x_1 + 3x_2 + 2x_3 \leq 10 \qquad \text{(constraint 1)}$$
$$x_1 + 3x_3 \leq 12 \qquad \text{(constraint 2)}$$
$$x_1, x_2, x_3 \geq 0.$$

The first step is to enter this problem in Excel in such a way that the decision variables, the objective value and the constraint values are in separate cells. See Figure 6.3 for a possible implementation of the above problem. For the decision variables we used arbitrary values $(1, 2, 3)$.

	A	B	C	D	E	F
1		Decision variables				
2		1	2	3		
3		Profit			objective	
4		2	4	8	34	
5	Constraint					
6	number	matrix			values	limits
7	1	1	3	2	13	10
8	2	1	0	3	10	12

Figure 6.3: LO implementation in Excel

The following formulas were entered:
- cell E4: =SUMPRODUCT(B$2:D$2,B4:D4)
- cell E7: =SUMPRODUCT(B$2:D$2,B7:D7)
- cell E8: =SUMPRODUCT(B$2:D$2,B8:D8)

Thanks to the $-signs, the formula only has to be entered once and can then be copied.

We are now ready to open the solver dialog. After entering the right values the dialog should look like Figure 6.4. The dialog can look slightly different, depending on your version of Excel. Hitting "Solve" will now solve the problem to optimality, with objective value 34.67.

Exercise 6.4 *Solve the problem of Exercise 6.2 using Excel. Note that the constraints can be entered one by one each having a different sign.*

Exercise 6.5 *The tax office can only check a subset of the tax declarations it received. There are 3 types of employees with different skills, and 3 types of declarations. Per declaration type, the expected revenues from additional taxation are as follows: $(200, 1000, 500)$ Euros. Every tax employee can process every declaration, except for employee type 2 who cannot process declaration type 2 and employee* *type 3 who cannot process declaration type 3. The time per declaration depends on the declaration type and is* $(1, 3, 2)$ *hours, respectively, except for employee type 3 who takes 2 hours for a type 1 declaration. The numbers of declarations are* $(15000, 6000, 8000)$, *the numbers of available hours are* $(10000, 20000, 15000)$. *How do you assign the employees to the different declaration types? Use Excel to solve this problem.*

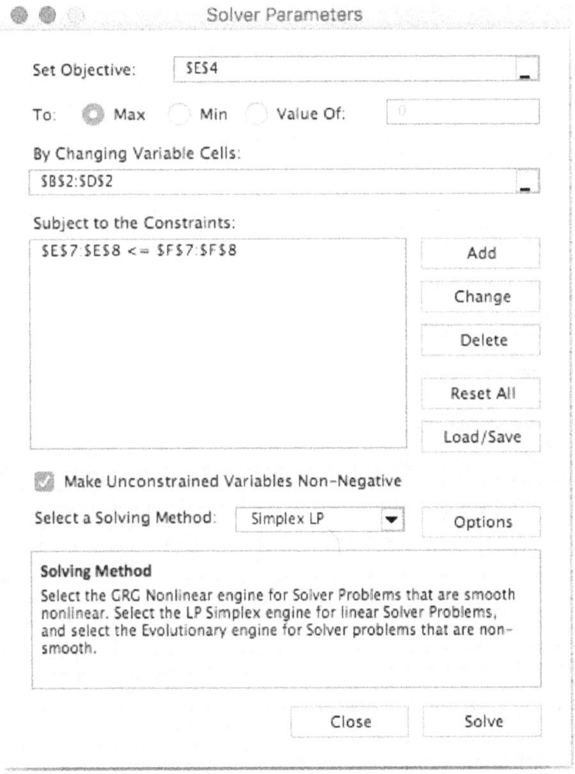

Figure 6.4: Excel solver dialog

The standard Excel solver is rather limited in capabilities. A simple alternative is the "OpenSolver" which is easy to install and comparable in use, but comes with a stronger solver without limitations on the numbers of variables or constraints. See OpenSolver.org.

Exercise 6.6 *Extend the problem of Figure 6.3 in the following ways. When solving these problems it helps to think what the additional decision is that needs to be* *taken.*

a. Assume that, next to the 10 units available, you can buy extra units of resource 2 for the price of 1 per unit. What is the optimal solution now?

b. The same question, but now you can buy resource 1 for 2 per unit.

c. The same question, but now you can buy resource 1 for 1 per unit. Can you interpret the result?

6.3 Example LO problems

In this section we consider several types of optimization problems that can be solved using LO.

A *graph* is the mathematical name for a network consisting of *nodes* and *edges* connecting the nodes. Nodes are sometimes also called *vertices*. Edges can be *directed* or *undirected*, i.e., uni-directional or bi-directional. Directed edges are often called *arcs*. Many practical problems can be formulated as problems on graphs. One such problem is *project planning*.

A project consists of a number of activities, each having a *duration*. These are the nodes in the graph. Additionally, certain activities require others to finish before they can get started. These precedence relations are modeled as directed edges in the graph. In Figure 6.5 an example of such a graph is given. We need to determine the earliest finish time of each activity. These are the decision variables, x_i for activity i. Every precedence relation leads to a constraint. When i precedes j then this can be enforced by the constraint $x_i + d_j \leq x_j$, where d_j is the duration of activity j. For example, in the project of Figure 6.5 we model the relation $F \rightarrow G$ by the constraint $x_F + 2 \leq x_G$.

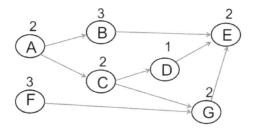

Figure 6.5: Directed graph with weights of a project planning problem

We are interested in the time at which all activities are finished. This can be modeled by an additional variable z, bigger than all finish times, that has to be minimized. This leads to the following LO formulation:

minimize z

subject to

$z \geq x_i$ for all vertices i

$x_i + d_j \leq x_j$ if i precedes j

$x_i \geq d_i$ for all vertices i.

The last constraint ensures that no activity starts before time 0. Note that the finish time can also be found using an algorithm without LO, and that this algorithm can be extended to random activity durations. This is relevant in practice because often durations are hard to predict accurately, which is one of the main reasons why, for example, IT projects often finish after the scheduled deadline.

Exercise 6.7 *Formulate the project planning problem of Figure 6.5 as LO problem and solve it using Excel.*

A more complicated problem that can be solved using LO is the so-called *transportation problem*. In this problem we have to transport a single type of good from n sources to m destinations. Source i has supply a_i, destination j has demand b_j, and link $i \rightarrow j$ has transportation costs c_{ij} per unit transported on it. The question is: For each link, how much should you ship on it in order to satisfy the demand of each destination without violating supply constraints? See Figure 6.6 for an illustration. When link $i \rightarrow j$ does not exist we can take $c_{ij} = \infty$.

The LO formulation is as follows:

$$\text{minimize} \sum_{i=1}^{n} \sum_{j=1}^{m} c_{ij} x_{ij}$$

subject to

$$\sum_{j=1}^{m} x_{ij} \leq a_i \text{ for } i = 1, \ldots, n;$$

$$\sum_{i=1}^{n} x_{ij} \geq b_j \text{ for } j = 1, \ldots, m;$$

$x_{ij} \geq 0$ for all i, j.

Exercise 6.8 *Solve the following transportation problem, where "x" means there is no connection.*

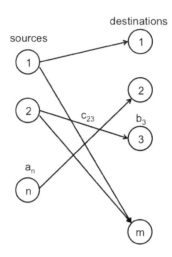

Figure 6.6: Transportation problem

i	a_i	$j = 1$	2	3	4
		c_{ij}			
1	10	0	5	x	0
2	3	6	4	6	4
3	6	2	10	2	4
4	6	6	x	4	6
	b_j	5	5	5	5

If we add intermediate nodes to the transportation problem, as in Figure 6.7, then we obtain the *transshipment problem*. We can solve it by adding constraints of the form:

$$\sum_{i=1}^{n} x_{ik} = \sum_{j=1}^{m} x_{kj}$$

for all intermediate nodes k. It can be extended to a network by adding multiple layers of intermediate nodes.

Next we consider *multi-period production/inventory models*. Here we assume there are multiple time periods, say $t = 1, \ldots, T$, and a starting inventory s_0. Every day, the amount of production or supply has to be decided: x_t. There is demand, d_t at time t, holding costs h_t, and production costs c_t. The problem is to find the production/order schedule that minimizes the total costs. This can be formulated as an LO problem as follows:

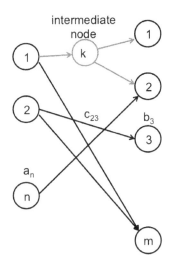

Figure 6.7: Transshipment problem

$$\text{minimize} \sum_{t=1}^{T}(c_t x_t + h_t s_t)$$

subject to

$$s_{t+1} = s_t - d_{t+1} + x_{t+1} \text{ for } t = 1, \ldots, T - 1;$$
$$x_t, s_t \geq 0 \text{ for } t = 1, \ldots, T.$$

This model can be extended in many different directions, such as maximum stock or production capacity, multiple products and resources, backorders, and fixed order costs (see Exercise 6.19).

6.4 Integer problems

For the simplex algorithm to be used, it is essential that the objective and all constraints are linear. Many extensions exist to non-linear functions. One important class is where there is, in addition to the linear constraints, constraints requiring one or more of the decision variables to be integer (i.e., taking values in $\{0, 1, 2, \ldots\}$) or binary (taking values in $\{0, 1\}$). We call these *integer linear optimization* (ILO) problems.

Note that binary problems are special cases of integer problems: the constraint $x_i \in \{0, 1\}$ is equivalent to the following 2 constraints: $x_i \in \{0, 1, 2, \ldots\}$ and $x_i \leq 1$.

Product-mix problems where we have to produce integer numbers of items is a good example. In R we can add an additional argument to the solver call:

```
> lp ("max", f.obj, f.con, f.dir, f.rhs, all.int=TRUE)
```

In Excel we have to add additional constraints, as in Figure 6.8.

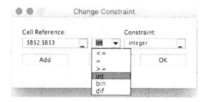

Figure 6.8: Entering integer and binary constraints in Excel

Exercise 6.9 *Solve the integer version of the problem of Section 6.1.*

The archetypical binary LO problem is the *knapsack problem*. You have to make a selection out of a set of items. Each item has a revenue and a weight. The goal is to maximize the total revenue with a constraint on the total weight. Typical applications of the knapsack are logistics problems, for example selecting items which have to be transported in trucks, or so-called cutting problems, which arise, for example, in steel plants where you have to cuts plates in pieces of different sizes.

As an example, consider a problem with total weight capacity 11. The items are as follows:

revenue	60	60	40	10	20	10	3
weight	3	5	4	1.4	3	3	1

Formulated as ILO we get:

maximize $60x_1 + 60x_2 + 40x_3 + 10x_4 + 20x_5 + 10x_6 + 3x_7$

subject to

$3x_1 + 5x_2 + 4x_3 + 1.4x_4 + 3x_5 + 3x_6 + x_7 \leq 11$

$x_i \in \{0, 1\}$ for all i.

Solving this using R or Excel leads to the optimum $(1, 1, 0, 0, 1, 0, 0)$ with value 140.

Exercise 6.10 *Verify that this is indeed the optimal solution by solving the problem in R and Excel.*

Although the solver seemed to have found the optimal answer without any problems, it required much more work. This becomes apparent when we solve big real-life ILO problems with hundreds or thousands of variables. To gain more insight in how ILOs are solved, let us have a look at Figure 6.9, where we see the steps to solve the knapsack example. We start with solving the LO *relaxation,* which is the problem without the integer or binary constraints (step 1). Sometimes we find an integer solution right away. Certain types of problems are even guaranteed to give integer solutions immediately. Here however x_3 is non-integer. Its value (150) is an upper bound to the best integer solution.

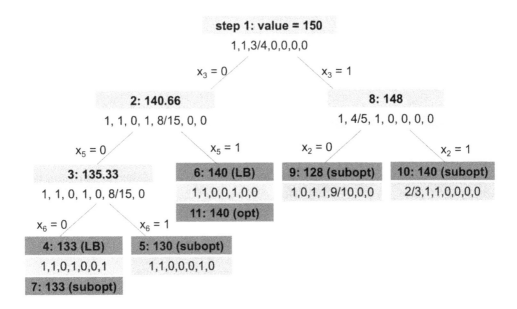

Figure 6.9: Solving an ILO problem

Now we *branch* on x_3, and we continue with the branch $x_3 = 0$. We solve the relaxation again, but with $x_3 = 0$. We find again a non-integer solution (step 2). We continue branching until we find an integer solution in step 4 with value 133. It is called a *lower bound* (LB) of the optimum: perhaps there are other integer solutions with values between 133 and 150. To find out if there are any such solutions we work our way back up to make sure all branches are dealt with. In step 5, we find an integer solution that is worse than the LB. In step 6, we find a higher binary value than the LB. It becomes the new LB, and the old LB is now sub-optimal (step 7). We have dealt with the left side of the tree, we move to the right. In step 8, we find a non-integer solution, we branch on x_2. In step 9 and 10, we find non-integer solutions which are worse or equal than the LB. Adding constraints will not make the value higher, therefore these branches can be discarded. We have dealt with all branches, and therefore the current LB is the optimum (step 11). This algorithm is called *branch-and-bound*.

Many LO solvers can also handle integer constraints. However, not all solvers can solve big instances. The best solvers are proprietary, notably CPLEX and Gurobi.

Exercise 6.11 *Solve by branch-and-bound the knapsack problem having rewards* $(15, 9, 10, 5)$, *sizes* $(1, 3, 5, 4)$ *and capacity 8. Check the result with R.*

6.5 Example ILO problems

In this section we discuss a number of problems that can be solved with ILO. The first is the *set cover problem*. We have a so-called *universe* $U = \{1, , \ldots, m\}$, and sets $S_1, \ldots, S_n$, with $S_i \subset U$. We are looking for the smallest selection of sets that covers U.

As an example, let U be set of locations where incidents can happen, and every set S_i the set of locations that can be reached by an ambulance from a certain base station within a certain target time. Then the set cover problem is as follows: what is the minimum number of ambulances needed and what are their base stations such that all locations can be reached within the target time?

The ILO formulation is as follows:

$$\text{minimize} \sum_{i=1}^{n} x_i$$

subject to

$$\sum_{i: u \in S_i} x_i \geq 1 \text{ for all } u \in U;$$

$$x_i \in \{0, 1\} \text{ for all } i.$$

The binary constraints are necessary, as the following example shows. Let $U = \{1, 2, 3\}$ and $S_1 = \{1, 2\}$, $S_2 = \{1, 3\}$, and $S_3 = \{2, 3\}$. Then any combination of 2 sets is optimal but the LO relaxation has optimal value 1.5 with solution $(0.5, 0.5, 0.5)$.

The main constraint is often replaced by the following more convenient notation: $\sum_{j=1}^{n} a_{uj} x_i \geq 1$ with $a_{uj} = 1$ if $u \in S_j$, 0 otherwise.

Exercise 6.12 *Solve the following ILO problem, inspired by [13]. A swimming pool is open during 12 hours, and the lifeguards at duty should be selected. Every lifeguard has his/her own working hours and wage, as given in the table. Select the optimal combination of lifeguards assuring at least 1 lifeguard at every moment. The hours mentioned are the first and last hour that each lifeguards works, thus Ben/Celia/Fred is a feasible solution.*

Lifeguard	Ann	Ben	Celia	Dick	Estelle	Fred
Hours	1–6	1–4	5–8	7–10	7–12	9–12
Wages	8	6	6	3	7	3

Solve it in Excel and use the SUMPRODUCT *function and a matrix with the values of* a_{ui}.

A generalization of the set cover problem is the *covering problem*. Instead of having to cover each element of the universe by 1 it can be more general. This leads to the following problem formulation:

$$\text{minimize} \sum_{i=1}^{n} x_i$$

subject to

$$\sum_{i=1}^{n} a_{ui} x_i \geq b_u \text{ for all } u \in U;$$

$$x_i \in \mathbb{N}_0 = \{0, 1, 2, \ldots\} \text{ for all } i.$$

This problem can be applied to *shift scheduling*, a problem already introduced by Dantzig in [7]. In shift scheduling, we have to find the best combination of shifts of employees, which in total cover the required workforce in every time interval. The seminal problem studied by Dantzig involved employees at a toll station, where the required coverage fluctuates during the day.

To model this as a covering problem, let U be the set of time intervals. Every set S_i corresponds to a shift (with $a_{ui} = 1$ meaning shift i works at time u), and b_u the number of required workers at time u. Then x_i corresponds to the number of employees that need to have shift i. By adding a coefficient to x_i in the objective we can add different costs to the shifts.

Exercise 6.13 *The required staffing in a call center, from 9am to 9pm in 30-minute intervals, is as follows:*
10, 11, 13, 16, 16, 13, 11, 10, 10, 11, 12, 13, 14, 14, 13, 11, 10, 9, 9, 10, 9, 8, 8, 8.
There are 2 types of shifts:
- 8 hours working time, with a 30-minute unpaid break in the middle, wage 20

Euro/hr, possible starting times every half hour from 9am to 12:30pm;
- 4 hours consecutive, wage 24 Euro/hr, possible starting times every half hour from 9am to 5pm.
    Formulate this as a covering problem and solve it with the Excel solver.

    Machine scheduling is another important class of ILO problems. However, because it involves some modeling tricks that are discussed in Section 6.7, we defer discussing it to that section.

    The next two exercises concern problems that can be solved with appropriately chosen binary decision variables.

Exercise 6.14 *For a day at a school, classes have to be assigned to professors such that each class has an hour with each required professor and such that there are no conflicts such as a professor having to teach two classes at the same time. A matrix with entries $a(c, p)$ indicates which classes need to have which professors: when $a(c, p) = 1$ then class c needs to have professor p, otherwise $a(c, p) = 0$.*

    Formulate an ILO model that minimizes the total number of hours that classes have to spend at school. A class remains at school until right after the last hour it has seen a professor.

Exercise 6.15 *For a classroom assignment, pairs need to be made of n students. Each student can give a list of students he or she is willing to work with.*

    Formulate an ILO model that maximizes the number of pairs that can be made. Each student is only allowed to be part of one pair, but it might not be possible to assign all students to a pair.

6.6   Modeling tools

So far we discussed solving LO and ILO problems, and the engines to solve them. However, we should realize that optimization specialists spend most of their time on *modeling*. Modeling is the translation of a real-life problem into a mathematical description that can be used to solve the problem. See Figure 6.10 for the steps in modeling. The time spent on modeling can be greatly reduced by using an appropriate modeling tool or language. As such, the existence of these modeling tools is considered to be of equal importance as the engines used to solve the models. To learn a modeling tool or language requires some time, but this easily pays off if you often build models for optimization problems.

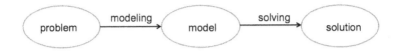

Figure 6.10: Modeling steps

The best known *algebraic modeling languages* (AMLs) are AIMMS, AMPL, GAMS, LINDO, and MPL. Some of these languages are part of an *integrated development environment* (IDE) that simplifies the modeling even further. The problem entry in these AMLs is quite similar to mathematical notation (see Box 6.2 on AMPL). Many of the tools and engines have free educational licenses, which makes it possible for students to learn and experiment. Even simpler to use is the *NEOS server*, a free cloud service which features a range of solvers to which one can submit optimization problems in a number of AML formats.

The AMLs and associated IDEs allow experienced modelers to model and solve problems they encounter. However, engines can also be built into software dedicated to solve a particular class of problems such as navigation software. These types of problem-specific tools are called *decision support systems* (DSSs). They are geared towards a different class of users. While AMLs are used by experienced data scientists and OR consultants, DSSs are most often used by planners with domain knowledge, but with less or no background in optimization and modeling.

6.7 Modeling tricks

In the previous section we saw which tooling to use. In this section we will see how to put problems in the (I)LO format. Thinking in the decision variables-objective-constraints framework often allows you to arrive at a problem formulation that resembles the standard (I)LO formulation. However, sometimes it is difficult to ensure that objective and constraints are linear. This section discusses some often-used tricks to formulate certain types of objectives and constraints in a linear way.

The first trick is useful when we want to minimize the absolute value of some decision variable, thus when the problem is of the form

$$\min\{c^T|x| \,|\, Ax \leq b\},$$

for some vector $c \geq 0$.

Box 6.2. A knapsack problem in AMPL

We give the AMPL implementation of the knapsack problem and a small instance which can be submitted right away to the NEOS server. The problem structure is implemented in the model file:

```
set ITEMS;

param size {ITEMS};
param total_size;
param revenue {ITEMS};

var take {ITEMS} binary;

maximize Total_Revenue:
        sum {i in ITEMS} take[i] * revenue[i];

subject to Size_Constraint:
        sum {i in ITEMS} take[i] * size[i] <= total_size;|
```

Next we need a data file in which the instance is given and finally the run file which tells the NEOS server what to do:

```
data;

set ITEMS := 1 2 3 4 5;

param: size :=
1   10
2   8
3   6
4   4
5   2;

param total_size := 15;

param: revenue :=
1   10
2   4
3   4
4   4                       solve;
5   1;                      display take;
```

Note that the problem structure and data are separated. When a planner has to solve a knapsack problem every day, he only needs to change the data file. Further details on the AMPL syntax can be found online or in the AMPL book [10].

The crucial idea is that the variable x_i can be rewritten as follows: $x_i = x_i^+ - x_i^-$ with $x_i^+, x_i^- \geq 0$ and one of them 0. Now the optimization problem can be rewritten as follows:

$$\min\{c^T(x^+ + x^-)\,|\,A(x^+ - x^-) \leq b, x^+, x^- \geq 0\},$$

which is linear. Because $c \geq 0$ for each i either $x_i^+ = 0$ or $x_i^- = 0$.

Exercise 6.16 *Numbers $a_1, \ldots, a_n$ are given. We are looking for x that minimizes $\sum_i |x - a_i|$. Formulate this as LO problem, and implement it in Excel for the following numbers: 1, 2, 3, 5, 8, 10, 20, 35, 100. How can you interpret the outcome?*

The previous exercise shows that the median minimizes the sum of absolute errors, much as the average minimizes the sum of squared errors. We can extend this to linear functions. We already did this for squared errors, for which *linear regression* is the method. For absolute errors it is called *quantile regression*. Points (x_i, y_i) are given and the objective is to find a function $y = a + bx$ such that the sum of absolute errors is minimized, see Figure 6.11.

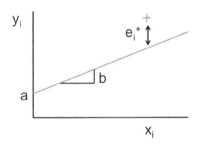

Figure 6.11: Quantile regression

In vector notation the problem can be formulated as follows:

$$\min\{\mathbf{1}^T |e| \mid y - (a\mathbf{1} + bx) = e\},$$

with $\mathbf{1}$ a vector with only 1's, and $e_i = y_i - (a + bx_i)$ the errors as given in the constraint. This can be made linear as follows:

$$\min\{\mathbf{1}^T (e^+ + e^-) \mid y - (a\mathbf{1} + bx) = e^+ - e^-, \quad e^+, e^- \geq 0\}.$$

We can generalize this to an asymmetric objective in the following way:

$$\min\{p\mathbf{1}^T e^+ + (1 - p)\mathbf{1}^T e^-) \mid y - (a\mathbf{1} + bx) = e^+ - e^-, \quad e^+, e^- \geq 0\},$$

with $0 < p < 1$. This explains the term quantile regression.

Exercise 6.17 *Consider Exercise 6.13. Assume we only have 8-hour shifts. To avoid overstaffing we replace the condition that staffing is met in every interval by the following objective: minimize the sum of absolute differences between demand and schedule. Formulate this as a LO problem and solve it using Excel.*

The next modeling trick is for cases where the objective function is not a sum but a maximum. The full problem is then of the form

$$\min\{\max\{x_1, \ldots, x_n\} \mid Ax \leq b, \ x \geq 0\}.$$

When discussing project planning we already say how this can be put in the LO framework:

$$\min\{z \mid z\mathbf{1} \geq x, \ Ax \leq b, \ x \geq 0\}.$$

Finally, there are some uses of a very big number, often called *big M*, in the context of ILO. The first is when an *indicator function* is part of the objective. An indicator function is a 0/1 function which is equal to 1 when a condition is satisfied. As an example, take the transportation problem with fixed costs K when a link is used. To model this, we introduce binary variables y_{ij} such that $y_{ij} = 1 \Leftrightarrow x_{ij} > 0$. Now we can simply add $K \sum_{i,j} y_{ij}$ to the objective function. But how to set y_{ij}? Here the value M comes into play, by adding the following constraints:

$$My_{ij} \geq x_{ij}.$$

We assume M is bigger than any x_{ij} ever can be. Thus, $x_{ij} > 0 \Rightarrow My_{ij} > 0 \Rightarrow y_{ij} = 1$. When $x_{ij} = 0$ then y_{ij} can be 0 or 1. Because we are minimizing costs and $K > 0$, y_{ij} will be 0. Thus $y_{ij} = 1 \Leftrightarrow x_{ij} > 0$.

Exercise 6.18 *Consider Exercise 6.8, but with an additional feature: every link that is used has fixed costs 5. Determine the optimal solution, using ILO.*

Exercise 6.19 *Consider the multi-period production/inventory model of page 94. Extend it to fixed order costs, meaning that costs K are incurred at t when $x_t > 0$, keeping all constraints linear.*

Big M can also be used in other situations, notably when a constraint only has to hold when a condition, which is part of the decision variables is satisfied. This condition is represented by a binary variable, let's say y, and the constraint is of the form $x \leq b$. Then a linear implementation is $x \leq b + (1 - y)M$. When $y = 0$ the contraint always holds because the right-hand side is very big. When $y = 1$ then we find the original $x \leq b$.

As an example, consider 2 jobs, A and B, that have to be executed consecutively, but the order is a decision to be made. Let x_A (x_B) be the starting time of job A (B), and d_A (d_B) the duration of A (B). When A goes before B then we get the condition $x_A + d_A \leq x_B$, otherwise $x_B + d_B \leq x_A$. This can be modeled in a linear way by having the following conditions:

$$x_A + d_A \leq x_B + (1 - y)M, \qquad x_B + d_B \leq x_A + yM, \qquad y \in \{0, 1\}.$$

Here $y = 1$ corresponds to A before B.

Exercise 6.20 *Assume that activities B and C of the project planning problem of Figure 6.5 use the same resource and therefore cannot be scheduled at the same time. Formulate this as ILO problem and solve it using Excel. The shortest finish time is 9.*

Machine scheduling   A problem in which several of these concepts occur is *machine scheduling*. We consider jobs that need to be scheduled on a single machine. Job i has release date r_i before which it cannot start, duration d_i, and due date t_i, $i = 1, \ldots, n$. The decision variable are x_i, when to start job i, and also binary variables y_{ij} with $y_{ij} = 1$ iff (read: if and only if) job i goes before j, for all $i \neq j$. We give all constraints and discuss objectives right after that:

$$x_i + d_i \leq x_j + My_{ji} \text{ for all } i, j \text{ such that } i \neq j, M \gg 0 \qquad \text{(overlap)}$$
$$y_{ij} + y_{ji} = 1 \text{ for all } i, j \text{ such that } i \neq j \qquad \text{(order)}$$
$$x_i \geq r_i \text{ for all } i \qquad \text{(release dates)}$$
$$y_{ij} \in \{0, 1\} \text{ for all } i, j \text{ such that } i \neq j$$

Different objectives are possible. Some common ones are:
- the *flowtime*, defined as $\sum_i (x_i + d_i - r_i)$, thus the sum of the times that the job is waiting to be processed or is being processed; that is, the time they spend "in the system";
- the *makespan*, defined as $\max_i \{x_i + d_i\}$, the time when the machine is ready with all jobs;
- the total *tardiness*, which is $\sum_i (x_i + d_i - t_i)^+$, the sum of the times that the jobs are late, counting finishing early as 0.

The makespan can be modeled by an additional decision variable z that needs to be minimized and which needs to satisfy: $x_i + d_i \leq z$ for all i.

The total tardiness can be modeled using additional decision variables z_i representing the tardiness of job i. The objective becomes $\min \sum_i z_i$, and we get additional constraints $x_i + d_i - t_i \leq z_i$ and $z_i \geq 0$ for all i.

The model quickly becomes big, also for moderate n: the number of variables is n^2, and the number of constraints is $2n^2 + n$.

Exercise 6.21 *Implement the single-machine scheduling problem with tardiness as objective in AMPL. Solve it for the following data with an appropriate solver on the NEOS server:*

duration	4	5	3	5	7	1	0	3	2	10
release time	3	4	7	11	10	0	0	10	0	15
due date	11	12	20	25	20	10	30	30	10	20

To implement a constraint that needs to hold for all i, j with $i \neq j$ you can use the following AMPL syntax:

```
subject to example_constraint {i in 1..N, j in 1..M: i<>j}:
```
2-dimensional binary variables are defined as follows:
```
var x {1..N, 1..M} binary;
```

Exercise 6.22 *Change the objective of Exercise 6.14 as follows: the time the last class finishes has to be minimized.*

6.8   Additional reading

Books on optimization come in two flavors: either they promote optimization to executives without going into any technical details (such as [35]), or they are written for students with a strong theoretical background such as industrial engineering. Books having a considerable overlap with the current chapters and containing many examples of optimization problems are introductions to MS/OR such as [17, 40, 42] and Rardin [32] which has a more narrow focus on deterministic optimization. Foreman [9] is another accessible book with some chapters on optimization (especially the last part of Chapter 1 and Chapter 4).

Project management is extremely important in practice and has many different scientific aspects. Project planning is one of these aspects which we only basically touched upon. A good starting point for further reading is Klastorin [21]. See also Section 5.1.

More details on the AMPL modeling language can be found in [10]. See en.wikipedia.org/wiki/List_of_optimization_software for a list of solvers. The NEOS server can be reached at neos-server.org/neos/. The AIMMS optimization modeling book [3] gives many modeling tricks.

In the presence of excellent LO and ILO solvers, much research effort is currently put into non-linear optimization. A a result, much progress has been made in this area over the last decade.

Chapter 7

Combinatorial Optimization

Combinatorics is the mathematical study of finite structures. *Counting problems* (e.g., how many ways are there to select k items out of n?) are a good example of a combinatorial problem. *Combinatorial optimization* (CO) considers optimization problems over these finite structures. Usually the number of elements is too big for the problem to be solved by enumeration. Therefore *algorithms* are at the heart of CO.

Integer linear optimization problems (see Chapter 6) with all variables integer have finite (or countable) feasible regions, but they are usually not considered to be part of CO. Together they constitute *discrete optimization*. As we will see, many CO problems have dedicated algorithms but can also be formulated as ILO problems. In the next sections we deal with a few of the most common CO problems. A common theme is *complexity*, which will be addressed in a separate section.

Learning outcomes   On completion of this chapter, you will be able to:

- solve certain combinatorial problems, especially the shortest path, the maximum flow and the traveling salesman problems

- describe the concept of complexity and reflect on its implications for algorithms and problem solving

7.1   The shortest path problem

The shortest path problem consists of finding the shortest distance between two nodes in a (uni or bi-directional) graph (see page 92) with (positive) distances on the arcs. The importance of this problem is evident: it has to be solved every time we use navigation software, and many other less obvious applications exist.

The best-known algorithm was invented by the Dutch computer scientist Edsger Dijkstra (1930-2002). His algorithm works as follows: let V be the set of nodes in the graph, and E the edges connecting them, and c_{ij} the distance from i to j. See Figure 7.1 for an example. Let s be the node from which we want to compute the shortest routes (Dijkstra calculates the shortest route to all nodes at the same time). The algorithm works as follows:

> initialization: $f(s) = 0$, $f(i) = \infty$ for all $i \in V \backslash \{s\}$,
> $\quad$ s is visited and current
> repeat until all nodes are visited:
> $\quad$ update all unvisited neighbors j of current node i, i.e., update
> $\quad\quad$ $f(j)$ to $f(i) + c_{ij}$ if $f(i) + c_{ij} < f(j)$
> $\quad$ determine unvisited node with smallest value
> $\quad$ make it visited and current

As an example let us determine the shortest path from A to F in the graph of Figure 7.1. When an edge is not present the distance is ∞. In Table 7.1 we see the algorithm step by step. Underlined numbers correspond to visited nodes.

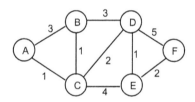

Figure 7.1: A graph with $V = \{A, B, C, D, E, F\}$ and distances along the edges

This algorithm terminates with $f(x)$ the shortest distance from s to j for any node j. Every time you update a node you can keep track of the minimizing arc. If you store this arc every time a node becomes visited, then you build a *tree* with the shortest paths to all nodes.

Exercise 7.1 *Find the shortest path from A to E for the graph in Figure 7.2 using Dijkstra's algorithm. Formulate it also as an LO problem using the formulation of the box below. Give the optimal solution and check its feasibility.*

step	A	B	C	D	E	F
			distances			
1	<u>0</u>	∞	∞	∞	∞	∞
2		3	<u>1</u>	∞	∞	∞
3		<u>2</u>		3	5	∞
4				<u>3</u>	5	∞
5					<u>4</u>	8
6						<u>6</u>

Table 7.1: Dijkstra's algorithm applied to the graph of Figure 7.1

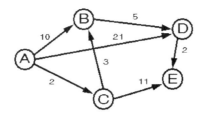

Figure 7.2: A directed graph with $V = \{A, B, C, D, E\}$ and distances along the arcs

---

Box 7.1. LO solution of shortest path problem

The shortest path problem can also be formulated as an LO problem. It is a special case of the transshipment problem of Section 6.3, with demand 1. We determine the shortest path from the source s to a single destination d. The LO formulation is as follows:

  minimize $\sum_{i \neq d} \sum_{j \neq s} c_{ij} x_{ij}$

  subject to

  $\sum_{j \neq s} x_{sj} = 1$;

  $\sum_{i \neq d} x_{ik} = \sum_{j \neq s} x_{kj}$ for all intermediate nodes $k \neq s$ and $k \neq d$;

  $x_{ij} \geq 0$ for all $i \neq j$.

Because there is only one destination d, the flow into it must be 1 and there is no need for a separate constraint. It can happen that the solution is non-integer, that the flow is split between multiple paths from s to d. In that case, every path with positive flow is optimal.

If we assume $c_{ij} = \infty$ if an arc does not exist then all summations can range over V.

Note that this formulation has n^2 variables and n constraints. Although LO problems can be solved efficiently, Dijkstra's algorithm is much faster.

It is interesting to look at the number of operations needed by Dijkstra, with $n = |V|$ the number of nodes. In every iteration of the algorithm, one node is made current; that makes n iterations. In every iteration all non-visited nodes are updated, that makes between $n - 1$ and 1 operations, depending on the iteration. Thus, the total number of operations $N(n) = c((n - 1) + (n - 2) + \cdots + 1) = cn(n - 1)/2$, with the c the (constant) number of operations to update one node. This is a second degree polynomial in n, therefore we say that N is *in the order of n^2*, written $N(n) = O(n^2)$. Formally, this means that $\lim_{n \to \infty} N(n)/n^2$ is a constant.

Exercise 7.2 *Implement the LO formulation of the shortest path problem in AMPL and use the NEOS server to solve the problem of Figure 7.1.*

Box 7.2. Navigation software

Dijkstra is essentially also the algorithm that is used in the software that is implemented in your TomTom software or in Apple or Google maps on your smartphone. However, when you calculate the shortest route from A(msterdam) to B(erlin), Dijkstra also computes roads to all other possible destinations which is highly inefficient.

Several solutions have been proposed in the literature to tackle this problem. We discuss a well-known one: the A* algorithm. It adapts Dijkstra's algorithm in the following way. An evaluation function $e(i)$ is introduced with $e(i) = f(i) + h(i)$, where $f(i)$ is the current distance from the origin to i and $h(i)$ is an estimation of the distance from i to the destination, for example based on the Euclidian distance (based on a straight line instead of the road network) and the maximum highway speed. Now the node with smallest value of $e(i)$ is made current. Under certain conditions ($h(i)$ must be smaller than the real distance) this new algorithm finds again the optimal route, and it is dramatically faster than Dijkstra.

7.2 The maximum flow problem

A second classic CO problem is the *maximum flow problem*. In a (possibly directed) graph we add a capacity to every edge. One node is the source, another node is the destination. The goal of the max flow problem is to transport as much as possible from source to destination using the edges of the graph without exceeding the maximal capacity on any edge. The Ford-Fulkerson algorithm was invented to solve this problem. It works as follows:

> initialization: assign flow of 0 to all arcs
> repeat:
>> find an *augmenting path*
>> add capacity of augmenting path to flow
> until no more augmenting path can be found

It needs to be specified how such an augmenting path can be found and how to determine and add its capacity. There are multiple ways to do this. We will not go into the technical details, instead we illustrate this graphically through an example which can be found as the upper-left graph in Figure 7.3. The source is A and the destination is F. Initially all flows are 0, thus the first augmenting path is simply a path in the graph from A to F, let's say A-B-D-F. The minimum capacity on the arcs is 2 (A-B), thus the capacity of the augmenting path is 2. We add this to the flow, leading to the upper-right graph of Figure 7.3.

We try to find a new augmenting path. We start from A. B cannot be reached, because its capacity is already fully used. C can be reached, from which we can reach B, D and E. From D we can reach F. This leads to the tree of the bottom-left graph, from which we derive the augmenting path A-C-D-F, with capacity 2 (because only 2 is left on D-F). After 2 more iterations we find the flow of the lower-right graph with value 6. When we try to find a new augmenting path we cannot reach E and F. Indeed, the sum of the capacities of the arcs from $\{A, B, C, D\}$ to $\{E, F\}$, called a *cut*, has value 6. There is a well-known theorem that states that the minimum over all cuts is equal to the maximum flow. Because we found a flow and a cut of 6 we are sure to have found an optimal solution.

Exercise 7.3 *Determine the maximum flow from A to H in the undirected graph of Figure 7.4. Check that there is a cut with the same value. Determine the optimal solution by implementing the LO solution in AMPL and/or Excel.*

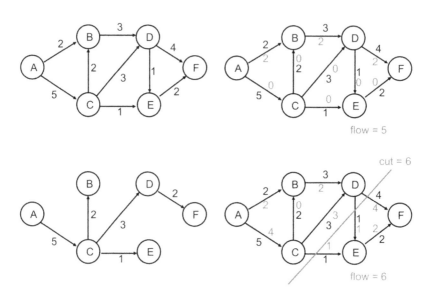

Figure 7.3: Ford-Fulkerson illustrated

Box 7.3. LO solution of maximum flow problem

Also the max flow problem can be formulated as LO problem. The objective is to maximize the flow out of the source s such that capacity constraints are not violated and all intermediate nodes have flow in = flow out.

maximize $\sum_{j \neq s} x_{sj}$

subject to

$x_{ij} \leq c_{ij}$ for all $i, j, i \neq j$;

$\sum_{i \neq d} x_{ik} = \sum_{j \neq s} x_{kj}$ for all intermediate nodes $k \neq s$ and $k \neq d$;

$x_{ij} \geq 0$ for all $i, j, i \neq j$.

Note that there are $n(n-1)$ variables and $2n(n-1) + n - 2$ constraints, with n the number of nodes in the network. Note also that these are 2nd order polynomials in n.

7.3 The traveling salesman problem

The third famous problem we consider is the *traveling salesman problem* or TSP. For an undirected graph with distances on the edges the objective is to visit all the nodes or cities in a closed *tour* with minimal total distance without visiting the same node twice. For example, if the numbers in Figure 7.4 are interpreted as distances, then the tour that visits the cities in a clockwise or counter-clockwise manner has distance 21. See the left graph of Figure

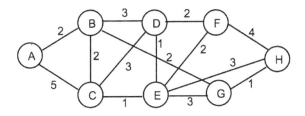

Figure 7.4: An undirected graph with capacities

7.5. However, it is possible to find shorter tours. Note that it doesn't matter which node is taken as a starting point because we have to return to that point anyway.

For the TSP, no efficient algorithm is known; essentially only enumeration is guaranteed to find the shortest tour. However, there are $(n-1)!$ different tours, which will take very long even for moderately sized problems! Therefore the TSP is solved using *heuristics*, i.e., algorithms that are not guaranteed to terminate with an optimal solution.

An example of such a heuristic is *2-opt*. It starts with some initial tour and then one by one all combinations of 2 edges are removed from the tour and replaced by the other 2 edges connecting them in order to make a tour again. When an edge does not exist, we assume it has length ∞. When the length of the new tour is shorter, we consider it as our next solution. This continues until no improvement can be found.

Let us apply this to the graph of Figure 7.4. We start with the left tour of Figure 7.5 which has length 21. If we replace the edges BD and EG we get the right graph of Figure 7.5 with length 18. No further improvements can be found.

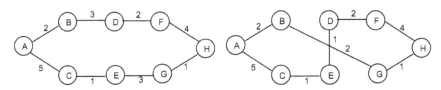

Figure 7.5: An illustration of the 2-opt heuristic

The final tour of the algorithm is called a *local optimum*, because in the *neighborhood* of the final tour there is no better solution, but there is no guarantee that the solution is optimal. An overall best solution (there can be more than one) is called a *global optimum*. The right-hand graph is a local optimum with respect to the 2-opt heuristic. It is also the global optimum.

Other heuristics than 2-opt exist, for example *3-opt*, which evidently consists of removing 3 edges from a tour and trying all the ways of reconnecting to make a tour again. These heuristics are also called *local search* methods: from a possible solution a *neighborhood* of solutions is defined which are searched. When a better one is found then it replaces the current one and the search continues from the new solution until no improvement can be made anymore. In the case of 2-opt the neighborhood of a tour consists of all tours that can be constructed from omitting 2 edges and adding the 2 edges which make the tour complete again. The quality of the local optimum depends strongly on the choice of neighborhood. For example, 3-opt is known to give better solutions than 2-opt.

Exercise 7.4 *Construct a local optimum using 2-opt for the graph of Figure 7.6 starting with the tour ABDFEC.*

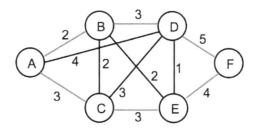

Figure 7.6: An undirected graph with distances

An R package "TSP" exists by which we can solve TSP problems.

Exercise 7.5 *Install the R TSP package, read the manual and use it to solve the problem of Figure 7.4.*

7.4 Complexity

In the previous sections we studied 3 archetypical CO problems: shortest path, max flow, and TSP. We saw a crucial difference between them: shortest path and max flow have run times polynomial in the size of the problem, but TSP grows as a factorial in n (which is faster than exponential). This really makes a difference. The following table illustrates that.

> **Box 7.4. ILO solution of the TSP**
>
> We can try to construct an LO formulation for the TSP, just like we did for the shortest path and the max flow problem. With c_{ij} we denote the length of the edge between i and j and x_{ij} is the binary variable which indicates whether the edge ij is included in the tour. Then the obvious LO formulation is:
>
> minimize $\sum_{i,j,i\neq j} c_{ij} x_{ij}$
>
> subject to
>
> $\sum_{i\neq k} x_{ik} = \sum_{j\neq k} x_{kj} = 1$ for all nodes k;
>
> $x_{ij} \in \{0,1\}$ for all $i, j, i \neq j$.
>
> However, this problem we does not always result in a tour. For example, when applied to the graph of Figure 7.6, we get two disconnected tours with 3 nodes: ABC and DEF. Therefore we need additional constraints, for example requiring that any subset has fewer used edges than there are nodes in the subset:
>
> $\sum_{i,j \in S} x_{ij} \leq |S| - 1$ for all $S \subset V$ with $2 \leq |S| \leq n - 2$.
>
> By adding this constraint, we can solve the TSP to optimality. However, there are 2^n subsets of V, leading to an exponential number of constraints. This makes this solution approach practically infeasible.

n	n^2	n^3	2^n	$n!$
10	100	1000	1024	3.6×10^6
100	10^4	10^6	1.3×10^{30}	9.3×10^{157}
1000	10^6	10^9	1.1×10^{301}	4.0×10^{2567}

If a solution takes 1 μs to evaluate, then an algorithm with n^3 steps takes 1 second to evaluate for size 100; an algorithm with $n!$ steps would take many times the age of the earth... Even if Moore's law, which roughly states that computer power doubles every two years, continues to hold, it will take thousands of years before hardware is fast enough to make running times acceptable.

Researchers are therefore always interested in finding an algorithm with polynomial *complexity*. For some problems (such as shortest path and max flow) these algorithms are found and mathematically proven to terminate with the optimal solution. For a group of other problems (such as the TSP) hundreds of researchers spend decades of their lives looking in vain for polynomial algorithms... This suggests that there are, roughly speaking, two classes of problems. P is the class of problems for which polynomial-time algorithms are known. NP-complete is a class of problems for which you can easily decide whether a proposed solution is indeed a solution, but for which there is no known polynomial-time algorithm to find the optimal solution. Shortest path and max flow are in P; TSP is an example of an NP-complete problem. Other NP-complete problems are the knapsack problem, machine scheduling and set covering.

Box 7.5. Complexity of linear optimization

The simplex method, which is the original method invented by Dantzig for solving LO problems, has been proven to work very well, even for very big problems. However, it is possible to construct problems for which the run time is not polynomial in the size, thus the simplex method is not in P. In the 1980s, the so-called *interior-point methods* were developed that solve LO in polynomial time. These are widely used since then.

It is important to note that there are more difficult classes of problems than NP-complete problems, for example those where it is hard to verify whether a proposed solution is indeed feasible. Note also that solving a mathematical optimization problem is only part of solving business problems. Indeed, translating a business problem into a mathematical model—*modeling*—is often harder than solving the resulting model. It is the ultimate goal of business analytics to solve any business problem in a rational data-driven way. Many of these problems, especially the strategic ones ("which product to develop?" or "how to maximize profit while keeping the risk of a loss below 5%?", or even "which employees to hire?") are very hard to model. Therefore modeling is an essential part of business analytics. Solving these types of problems in a rational mathematical way was the promise of management science in the 1950s. This failed and OR/MS was largely focused on operational problems in the following decades. The availability of data brings the solution to these problems within reach.

7.5   Additional reading

It is hard to find easily accessible books on CO. Standard introductions to operations research such as [17, 40, 42] discuss network models, but only Taha [40] discusses the TSP, and none complexity of algorithms.

The A* algorithm was introduced in Hart el al. [15]. Schultes [37] contains the methods currently used in route planning software.

For formal definitions of P, NP-complete and other concepts such as NP-hard we refer to Papadimitriou & Steiglitz [28]. Wikipedia is also a good starting point.

Chapter 8

Simulation Optimization

Up to now we considered optimization problems that involved no randomness. However, few problems in practice are completely predictable. Although sometimes replacing random variables by constants can give a decent approximation, it can also result in very wrong results, as we saw in the project planning example on page 78.

In Chapter 9 we study dynamic decision problems, in which multiple decisions have to be taken, and where each decision has partially unpredictable consequences for the future. In this chapter we consider once-off decisions, where the value of every solution can only be obtained through simulation. This has important implications for optimization: you are never sure if one solution is better than another, unless you simulate many times. However, this might be very time-consuming, especially when there are many possible solutions. In this chapter, we discuss methods to deal with this problem.

Different names are used for this method: simulation optimization, optimization by simulation, simulation-based optimization, or simply simopt.

Learning outcomes On completion of this chapter, you will be able to:

- describe the concept of simulation optimization and its various methods

- reflect on its usefulness for solving business problems with various options and uncertain outcomes

- solve certain simple problems using R or Excel

8.1   Introduction

In this chapter we bring together two concepts from previous chapters: randomness and decisions. Because we used the variable x for both these concepts in previous chapters, we have to change the notation: we will use π for the decision. The problems we study in this chapter are of the form $\max \mathbb{E}r(\pi, X)$ with $\pi \in S$ and with the additional feature that we can only approximate $\mathbb{E}r(\pi, X)$ using simulation.

Example 8.1 *The examples from Chapter 5 can be extended to incorporate decisions: the impact of strategic decisions of a company can be compared in the budget using simulation; the process in the emergency department of a hospital can be optimized using simulation, etc.*

Example 8.2 *A common and simple stochastic optimization problem is the* newsvendor problem. *A newsvendor who has to buy newspapers every morning. During the day he or she sells them. Remaining newspapers at the end of the day are worthless and have to be discarded. The newsvendor has to decide how many newspapers to buy in the morning. Because demand is random, there is a risk of lost revenue and of costs for papers that are left over. What is the optimal order size if the objective is to maximize expected profit?*

For a problem like the newsvendor we could simulate each solution a number of times and make confidence intervals. However, there are a number of problems with this approach. What does it mean if the CIs are non-overlapping? Or only overlapping for a small part? Furthermore, there may be so many solutions that this approach is infeasible from the beginning. And even if it is feasible, we want to concentrate on possible winners and discard solutions with really low values from the beginning. In the next sections we will discuss methods for all these issues, depending on the form of S.

Box 8.1. Random constraints

We could generalize the problem formulation even further, from $\max \mathbb{E}r(\pi, X)$ with $\pi \in S$ to $\max \mathbb{E}r(\pi, X)$ with $\mathbb{E}g_j(\pi, X) \leq b_j$, thereby introducing random constraints. Although we will encounter a number of such problems, we will focus on the case $\pi \in S$. Problems with random constraints are very hard to solve.

S can be of two basic forms: discrete or continuous, i.e., for example of the form $[0, 1]$ or of the form $\{0, 1, 2, \ldots\}$. We will focus on discrete problems.

Note that a continuous S can always be made discrete: instead of $[0,1]$ we could consider $\{0, 0.01, 0.02, \ldots, 1\}$.

For S discrete we discuss 3 separate methods, for the following cases:
- $|S| = 2$;
- $|S|$ small;
- $|S|$ big or even infinite.

8.2 Comparing scenarios

The simplest form of optimization is when $|S| = 2$, when we compare two *scenarios* to see whether the objective value of one is higher or lower than the other. In this situation we typically perform an equal number of runs of both situations. Then we make a CI of the differences. If this CI excludes 0 then we have evidence that one scenario is better than the other.

Exercise 8.1 *We extend Exercise 5.3 on page 79 with a second product. Management has to decide between both products. All variables are again normally distributed, with mean and SD 12000 and 2000 for sales; 90 and 20 for the price; 68 and 20 for the variable costs; 165000 and 30000 for the fixed costs.*
a. Simulate both scenarios 10000 times and make a CI for the difference. Which one is better? Explain your answer.
b. Do the same time, but using common random numbers (as in Box 8.2). What is the difference?

8.3 Ranking and selection

In this section we consider problems for which the number of solutions is finite and limited in size, allowing us to simulate every possible solution multiple times.

Example 8.3 *A well-known problem of this type is the* newsvendor problem *of Example 8.2. Let X be the random demand; π the order size; p the selling price; and c the purchasing price. For given demand x, the profit is equal to $p \min\{x, \pi\} - c\pi$. By simulating the demand, we can simulate the profit and determine the expected profit per order size level. Possible values for π are $0, 1, 2, \ldots$ up to a certain level, for example the maximum shelf space.*

Box 8.2. Common random numbers

It might take a long computation time to get a tight CI, especially in the case of complicated discrete-event simulations. Sometimes the variability of the differences between the scenarios can be reduced by a technique called *common random numbers*. The idea is that for random variables that are used in both scenarios, the same outcomes are taken. As a result the runs become dependent, and often the variability is reduced. For example, in a service center where we change the service delivery process, we might take the same customer arrival moments for both scenarios. This often reduces drastically the variance and therefore also reduces the width of the CI. This method is illustrated in the figures below: the left shows two independent traces with a small difference in process; the right shows the same random traces but with common random numbers.

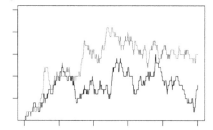 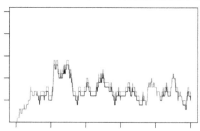

Exercise 8.2 *Consider a newsvendor problem with demand Poisson distributed with average 15, $p = 1$, $c = 0.75$, and $\pi \in S = \{1, 2, \ldots, 50\}$.*

a. Simulate the expected demand 1M times for each value of π and determine the optimal π and its value.

b. Now we only can do 5000 simulations in total. Split these equally over S and determine the highest value and the corresponding π. Repeat this a number of times and observe what happens.

From this exercise, we see two major disadvantages to simopt: because of the noise we might not recognize the signal and pick the wrong solution, and because of the noise we might overestimate the value: instead of selecting the solution with the highest value we pick the one with the highest random component. To avoid this we could simulate each solution much more times, but this might take too much time. Often we are restricted to a certain number of runs: the *simulation budget*. As a result, we cannot avoid the disadvantages completely, but we can improve upon an equally split simulation budget.

A smarter solution is to first simulate all solutions a limited number of times, and then discard solutions which are unlikely to be optimal. This selection is based on a statistical test. Therefore, for $|S| = k$ and a simulation budget of in total m runs, we first simulate each solution $m_0 < \lfloor m/k \rfloor$ times to have an initial estimation of the mean and its estimation error, by calculating the sample mean and variance of each solution. ($\lfloor \cdot \rfloor$ is the *floor* operator, meaning rounding down to an integer value.) Define the sample means and variances by $y(\pi)$ and $s^2(\pi)$.

When can we discard a solution π? When there are only 2 solutions π and π', we can discard π, using a 1-sided hypothesis test (see page 50), if:

$$y(\pi) < y(\pi') - \frac{1.64\sqrt{s^2(\pi) + s^2(\pi')}}{\sqrt{m_0}}.$$

Note that in R qnorm(0.95) is equal to 1.64.

Now we have $|S| - 1$ other solutions. The total probability of falsely discarding π should be 0.05. For each comparison it should be $1 - \sqrt[|S|-1]{0.95}$. For $|S| = 50$ this is equal to 0.001. In this case qnorm(0.999) gives 3.08.

This leads to the following set of candidate solutions:

$$I = \left\{ \pi \,\middle|\, y(\pi) > y(\pi') - \Phi^{-1}\left(\sqrt[|S|-1]{1-\alpha} \right) \frac{\sqrt{s^2(\pi) + s^2(\pi')}}{\sqrt{m_0}}, \ \pi' \neq \pi \right\}.$$

The remaining budget $m - m_0$ is equally split between the candidate solutions and the best is chosen.

Exercise 8.3 *Apply ranking and selection to the situation of Exercise 8.2 with a budget of 5000 simulations.*

8.4 Local search

If S is very large or even *countable* (e.g., $\{1, 2, \dots\}$) then we cannot start by simulating all $x \in S$ a number of times. In this situation there is often some structure that we can exploit. Just as in the case of deterministic local search (see page 114) we define a neighborhood $N(x)$ for every $x \in S$. During each iteration we randomly choose a point in the neighborhood of the current point and simulate both solutions once. Then we move to the best of the two and we iterate again. In more detail the algorithm is as follows:

Algorithm for local search simulation optimization
0. Set $n(\pi) = 0$ for all $\pi \in S$, choose π^*
1. Select randomly $\pi' \in N(\pi^*)$ and simulate π^* and π'
2. update averages $y(\pi^*)$ and $y(\pi')$, increase by 1 $n(\pi^*)$ and $n(\pi')$
3. If $y(\pi^*) < y(\pi')$ then $\pi' = \pi^*$
4. Repeat from 1 until simulation budget is exhausted
5. $\pi^* = \arg\max_\pi \{n(\pi)\}$

This is one of the simplest algorithms that exists. Many more elaborate algorithms are described in the scientific literature. Experience shows that the quality of the final solution is improved if the algorithm is repeated with different initial solutions.

Example 8.4 *In Chapter 6 (page 99) we discussed shift scheduling. There, the required capacity per interval was given. Often, the capacity in one interval has consequences on another, and simulation is the only tool to evaluate these effects. In such a situation, simopt can be used.*

Exercise 8.4 *Solve Exercise 8.3 using local search with a budget of 5000. Take $N(x) = \{x - 1, x + 1\}$ (unless $x = 1$ or 50, then N is 2 or 49). Make a plot of the current solution as the algorithm progresses. You can do this in Excel or R. Doing it in R requires the use of for-loops.*

8.5   Additional reading

There are few accessible books on simopt. Nelson [26] is a textbook on simulation that includes a chapter on simopt; Fu [11] is an accessible introduction to the subject.

Note that we have not discussed situations in which the solution space is continuous, for example all values between 0 and 1. In these situations approximations of derivatives (in more dimensions called *gradients*) are very useful.

Chapter 9

Dynamic Programming and Reinforcement Learning

This chapter discusses sequential decision problems, meaning that you have to take a series of actions where each action has a direct impact but also influences the future. The challenge is to estimate the future impact of your current action in order to make the right trade-off between current reward and future rewards. Possibly, you also have to learn about the problem parameters, introducing an additional trade-off between maximizing reward based on current knowledge (*exploitation*) or investing in discovering your environment (*exploration*).

This type of problem has been studied in the mathematical community since the 1950s under the name *dynamic programming*. The AI community has been studying similar problems under the name *reinforcement learning*, with more focus on learning and computational methods. It has a large number of possible applications, such as finding your way in a network, deciding on investment decisions, or setting the prices of airline tickets.

Reinforcement learning is considered to be the big promise of data science. But we will start with the classical theory of dynamic programming.

Learning outcomes   On completion of this chapter, you will be able to:

- describe the concepts of dynamic programming and reinforcement learning and its methods

- reflect on its usefulness and (future) potential for solving dynamic learning problems

- solve certain simple problems using R

9.1 Dynamic programming

Crucial in dynamic programming (DP) is the concept *state*. At any point in time, the *decision process* is in a state. Over time, this state changes depending on the actions taken and possibly depending on randomness. The state contains all information necessary to make future decisions, meaning no additional historical information can improve the decisions taken.

Example 9.1 *In a road network, the state might be the current location. In an investment application, it might be the current portfolio. When pricing and selling airplane tickets, it might be the number of remaining seats on a flight.*

At the same time, the state should be as concise as possible in order to make computations feasible. For example, when pricing airplane tickets, it makes no sense to add the revenue already obtained: that does not influence future rewards.

In a state, an action is chosen. The next state is determined by the (state,action)-pair, possibly involving randomness. At the same time a reward is obtained, and the whole process starts over again in the new state. This is repeated until the destination is reached or the airplane leaves.

The challenge is to find the *policy* that maximizes the total (expected) reward (or, when appropriate, minimizes total costs). A policy prescribes at any time in each state, which action to take. This problem was solved by Richard Bellman (1920-1984) in 1953. Together with the simplex algorithm for linear programming invented by George Dantzig (see Chapter 6), it is one of the two big inventions in OR in the 1950s.

Central in Bellman's DP algorithm is the so-called *value function*. It is the maximal reward-to-go when there are still t steps to go, in state $s \in S$, written as $V_t(s)$. Before giving the DP algorithm, we need two more definitions: when in state s action a is chosen, then the direct reward (or cost) is $r(s,a)$ $(c(s,a))$ and the next state is $\Gamma(s,a)$. Now we can recursively find the value function by computing the *Bellman equation*:

$$V_{t+1}(s) = \max_a \{r(s,a) + V_t(\Gamma(s,a))\}$$

or

$$V_{t+1}(s) = \min_a \{c(s,a) + V_t(\Gamma(s,a))\}.$$

With $\max_a\{\cdot\}$ we mean that we are looking for the action a that maximizes what is between brackets. Note that, starting from V_0, we compute V_1, V_2, etc. The subscript indicates the time-to-go. Therefore we work backwards in time, starting from the end of the horizon. For this reason DP is sometimes called *backward recursion*.

The standard textbook application of DP is the shortest path problem for which we already gave algorithms in Chapters 6 and 7. The state is the current node, and the action is the arc to travel on. The costs are the distances of the arcs, and $V_t(s)$ should be interpreted as the minimal distance from s to the destination d in at most t steps. As initial values, we set $V_0(d) = 0$ and $V_0(s) = \infty$ for all $s \neq d$. We also introduce the option to stay in a node, with distance 0. Now we can directly apply the Bellman equation, as is illustrated in the next example.

Example 9.2 *Let us determine the shortest path from A to F in Figure 7.1. We need to compute the value function; the results can be found in the table below. Note that the computation goes from top to bottom.*

V_0 is given. Now compute V_1. As an example,

$$V_1(D) = \min\{V_0(D), 3 + V_0(B), 2 + V_0(C), 1 + V_0(E), 5 + V_0(F)\} = 5.$$

Note that the first term, $V_0(D)$, comes from the fact that you can always stay in a state. When V_1 is computed, we continue with V_2, etc., until the numbers do not change anymore. V_5 gives the lengths of the shortest paths to F with an arbitrary number of steps. The minimizing actions give the shortest paths.

			shortest path to F			
t	A	B	C	D	E	F
0	∞	∞	∞	∞	∞	0
1	∞	∞	∞	5	2	0
2	∞	8	6	3	2	0
3	7	7	5	3	2	0
4	6	6	5	3	2	0
5	6	6	5	3	2	0

Exercise 9.1 *Verify all numbers in the table.*

Exercise 9.2 *Determine the shortest path to E in Figure 7.2 using DP. Do this by hand, in Excel and/or in R. The implementation in R requires programming experience.*

Box 9.1. Definitions of dynamic programming

The explanation provided earlier of DP is the common one in the mathematic community. In computing a more general definition is used: DP is a method in which problems are solved recursively by solving simpler subproblems. An example is Dijkstra's algorithm for the shortest path (see page 108). If node i is on the shortest path from s to d, then the shortest path from s to i is part of the shortest path from s to d. This property guarantees that the recursion in the algorithm indeed generates the shortest path to all nodes.

9.2   Stochastic Dynamic Programming

We can make the dynamic programming algorithm *stochastic* by replacing the deterministic transition Γ by a distribution on the states $\mathcal{S}$. Thus, if we choose action a in s, then we move to u with probability $p(s, a, u)$. The ps are called the *transition probabilities*, and of course $\sum_u p(s, a, u) = 1$ for all s and a.

Now V_t should be interpreted as the *expected* reward-to-go, and Γ should be replaced by the expectation over the possible future states:

$$V_{t+1}(s) = \max_a \{r(s, a) + \sum_u p(s, a, u) V_t(u)\}. \tag{9.1}$$

In matrix form it is $V_{t+1} = \max_\pi \{r(\pi) + P(\pi) V_t\}$, with π the $\mathcal{S}$-dimensional action vector.

Box 9.2. Markov decision processes

Stochastic dynamic programming was the name used by Bellman. Nowadays this scientific field is better known under the name *Markov decision processes*. The reason is as follows. If we omit the actions from the problem we get a process that moves from state to state according to probability distributions. These are called Markov chains or processes, after the Russian mathematician who introduced them. Adding actions makes it a *Markov decision process*. Markov chains are widely used in areas such as *queueing theory, inventory theory* and *performance analysis*.

We will show how this works with an example where we set the optimal prices for tickets of a flight. It is more intuitive to define t in V_t as time instead of time-to-go, thus we change the order of t. Now time t runs from 1 to T, the moment at which the flight departs. We assume that the time intervals are so short (say, 1 hour) that at most 1 ticket is sold during each interval (we disregard group bookings). The state s denotes the number of remaining seats. Demand fluctuates over time, and different customers have a different *willingness to pay*, being the maximum price they are willing to pay for the ticket.

There are N fares, $f(1) > \cdots > f(N)$. The demand at t with willingness to pay $f(n)$ is $d_t(n)$, with $\sum_{n=1}^{N} d_t(n) \leq 1$ for all t. Thus, when price $f(a)$ is offered at t, then with probability $\sum_{n=1}^{a} d_t(n)$ a ticket is sold. The value function of this problem is as follows, for $t < T$ and $s > 0$:

$$V_t(s) = \max_{a} \left\{ \sum_{n=1}^{a} d_t(n)\Big(f(a) + V_{t+1}(s-1)\Big) + \Big(1 - \sum_{n=1}^{a} d_t(n)\Big) V_{t+1}(s)\right\}.$$

Obviously, $V_t(0) = V_T(s) = 0$ for all t and s. Note that, in contrast with (9.1), the transition probabilities p also depend on t.

Example 9.3 *Consider a small hotel with 20 rooms and room prices of €500 and €200. There are 40 days in which bookings can be made. Demand for €200 is 0.5 every day, demand for €500 increases linearly from 0.01 to 0.4 over time. The optimal pricing strategy, computed using dp, is plotted in Figure 9.1.*

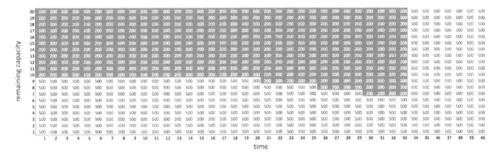

Figure 9.1: The optimal policy for the 20-room example

Exercise 9.3 *a. Explain intuitively the form of the optimal policy. Why is the lower price not offered the last weeks, even when there is ample capacity? And why does the capacity at which the lower price is offered decrease in the remaining time?*
b. In Excel, reproduce Figure 9.1 and determine the total expected revenue.
c. In R, determine the total expected revenue. This requires programming experience.

Box 9.3. Revenue management

Revenue management is one of the success stories of OR. Since the deregulation of the aviation markets in North-America and Europe airlines have been using it to maximize their revenues. Its goal is to maximize revenues in cases with fixed capacity and the possibility to change prices. It consists of a combination of forecasting and optimization. Revenue management, sometimes also called *yield management*, was first used by American Airlines to fight its main competitor at the time, the low-cost carrier People Express. As a result, People Express went bankrupt. Later it has also been applied to sectors such as hospitality and car rental. It has increased revenues by billions of Euros and made flying possible for large groups of people, including those with a limited budget.

Curse of dimensionality In hotels people sometimes book more than one night. If we want to compute the optimal price in this situation it is suboptimal to compute the value functions per night and sum the prices. For example, on a busy night we want to keep capacity free for people staying multiple nights, bringing additional income. To compute the optimal price for the whole stay, a multi-dimensional DP is needed, with the availabilities in different nights as state. A similar phenomenon occurs in aviation, where a journey might consist of multiple flight legs.

However, computing the optimal value for such a multi-dimensional state space is challenging. Suppose, for example, that we want to integrate pricing for a full week in our 20-room hotel. Then the size of the state space is $21^7 \approx 1.8 \times 10^9$, requiring at least 8GB to store V_t for only one value of t. To execute the DP recursion we need to store at least two of such value functions. When the capacity is bigger (few commercial airplanes have less than 100 seats), or the dimension higher (the networks of many airlines consist of 10s of possible connecting flights), then computation becomes impossible.

This is called the *curse of dimensionality*, and it was already recognized by Bellman in the 1950s. Only recently considerable progress has been made to circumvent this problem. In the next section we discuss such a method.

Discounted and long-run average reward Up to now, we discussed problems with a finite horizon T. However, unlike the departure of a plane, there are many situations for which there is no obvious moment to terminate. Think about managing an investment portfolio or the stock positions in a warehouse. In these situations, we cannot consider the total expected reward, because the sum over the infinite horizon will often be infinite. There are two options in these situations: either we consider the long-run average reward, or the *discounted* reward. For both there is an enormous amount of scientific literature, focusing mainly on convergence properties of policies and rewards. We will focus on discounted rewards: reward earned later in time is worth less than reward earned now. Discounting is exponential: reward R_t earned at t is worth $\alpha^t R_t$, with $0 < \alpha < 1$ the discount factor. Therefore the total discounted rewards are $\sum_{t=0}^{\infty} \alpha^t R_t$. Note that

$$\sum_{t=0}^{\infty} \alpha^t R_t = R_0 + \alpha \sum_{t=0}^{\infty} \alpha^t R_{t+1}.$$

This brings us to the following discounted DP recursion:

$$V_{t+1}(s) = \max_a \{ r(s,a) + \alpha \sum_u p(s,a,u) V_t(u) \}. \tag{9.2}$$

This recursion has a very interesting property: under quite general conditions V_t converges as $t \to \infty$ to some function V, called the discounted value function. From this, the optimal policy can be derived which is the same at every time (but of course different in different states).

Box 9.4. Multi-armed bandit problems

Bandit problems are multi-dimensional DP problems with a special structure. At any point in time one of the *arms* is selected, only rewards from that arm are obtained, and only this arm changes state according to its transition law. The problem is to decide at each time epoch which arm to pull, taking into account that sometimes you have to select an arm multiple times before you receive the reward worth pulling that arm. Moreover, as transitions are random, it is not clear whether they pay off and when you should switch arms. This multi-dimensional problem can be solved in multiple 1-dimensional problems, by calculating the *Gittins index* of every arm. This index can be interpreted as the expected discounted reward per unit of time of an arm, given its current state. Selecting the arm with the highest index is optimal.

Bandit problems can be applied to situations such as medical decision making (which treatment to choose) and portfolio decisions (which project or company to invest in).

9.3   Approximate Dynamic Programming

In the previous section we saw that the state can be so big that the value function cannot be computed, simply because it does not fit in memory.

Over the last few decades a new technique has come into existence to solve these type of problem: *approximate dynamic programming* (ADP). ADP is a ML-approach to DP: based on approximations of the value function in a number of states we fit a model. Hence the alternative name neuro-DP, suggesting the use of ANNs as machine learning technique. However, more often low-degree polynomials are taken, thus using linear regression.

The algorithm works as follows. You have to select a subset S' of the state space S and an *approximation architecture*, which is an ML model with the state components as attributes. We approximate V_t, which is a vector with a number in memory for every possible state, by W_{β_t}, which is a function of the parameters β_t of the ML model. Thus $W_{\beta_t}(s)$ can be easily computed while $V_t(s)$ cannot be stored in memory for all $s \in S$. Now you repeat the following steps starting with some arbitrary β_0:

1. $V_t(s) = \max_a \{r(s,a) + \alpha \sum_u p(s,a,u) W_{\beta_{t-1}}(u)\}$ for all $s \in S'$
2. determine the parameters β_t of the fit of V_t over S'

Note that from $s \in S'$ states outside of S' might be reachable, therefore we really need an approximation for the entire S.

Example 9.4 *A call center has multiple queues through which calls come in. Each queue may represent a different language or type of service request. Employees (often called* agents*) can handle different types of calls, depending on their skill set. How can you best assign calls to agents? This a difficult problem to solve, because in your assignments you have to take the impact on potential future arrivals into account. ADP can be used solve these type of problem; a linear approximation using squares of and interactions between queue lengths is typically a good choice.*

9.4   Models with partial information

Up to now we looked at models where r and P are completely known. From now on we consider systems where this is not the case, where information is obtained while operating the system. The challenge is to obtain information on the process (to *explore*) and to maximize discounted rewards (to *exploit*) at the same time. Basically there are two approaches to take: a statistical *Bayesian* one and a more computational heuristic approach. We start with the former, heuristics are discussed in Section 9.5.

We mentioned earlier that the state should contain all information to make future decisions. Following this reasoning, we should include all information about the unknown parameters in the state description as well.

Starting from some initial belief about the parameters, we update these beliefs every time we observe a transition. This typically leads to high-dimensional problems, but we can at least theoretically formulate a method to find the reward-optimizing policy.

Example 9.5 *Suppose a doctor has the choice between two treatments to which she has to sequentially assign her patients. Each time she updates her belief about the success probability of each treatment. This is a bandit problem (see Box 9.4 on page 129) with partial information about the success probabilities of both treatments.*

As a consequence, in the case that we learn about the transition probabilities, our beliefs on these transition probabilities should be part of the state. These beliefs take the form of distributions. This means that the state contains distributions of the transition probabilities and/or rewards. At every transition these distributions are updated, using a formula which is known as *Bayes' rule*. General distributions are hard to describe, therefore we prefer to use (families of) known distributions, characterized by a few parameters.

Example 9.6 *In the example with the treatments with unknown effect, the states are distributions on $[0,1]$. Every time the treatment with unknown effect is chosen, we move to another distribution, depending on the outcome. It is possible to reduce the number of possible states considerably. When our initial (a priori) belief is a uniform distribution, then our a posteriori belief, after any number of successes or failures, is a beta distribution. Beta distributions have only 2 integer parameters. An illustration of the transitions and the densities for 1 treatment can be found in Figure 9.2.*

Exercise 9.4 *Assume we have 1 treatment with known treatment success probability of 0.5 and 1 with a uniform prior. Read about the beta distribution on Wikipedia and implement the Bayesian learning algorithm in R or another appropriate language. Plot the optimal policy as a function of the number of successes and failures of the unknown arm.*
Simulate the process with unknown success probability equal to 0.4. Interpret the answers.
This exercise requires programming experience.

A great feature of the Bayesian approach is that it automatically makes the optimal trade-off between exploration and exploitation. The drawback is the dimensionality. Apart from very small problems such as the example given, it is generally impossible to compute the optimal policy. In these cases, we have to rely on suboptimal heuristics.

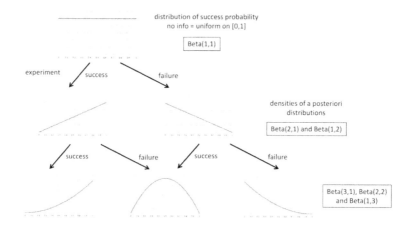

Figure 9.2: Changes of the information state for an initial uniform belief

9.5   Reinforcement Learning

In this section we study heuristics for partial-information problems, an important class of algorithms within reinforcement learning. To this end, we introduce a new concept—Q-values—and a new algorithm—Q-learning.

Because data arrives as we learn, we call this *online learning*; and because we directly estimate the value function without estimating parameters of some model as in the previous section, we call these methods *model-free*.

We first introduce the Q-values, which are defined for the standard *offline* DP method. Using V_t as in Equation (9.2) we define:

$$Q_{t+1}(s,a) = r(s,a) + \alpha \sum_u p(s,a,u) V_t(u).$$

Then the following recursion exists for these state-action values:

$$Q_{t+1}(s,a) = r(s,a) + \alpha \sum_u p(s,a,u) \max_b Q_t(u,b).$$

The advantage of computing the Q-values Q_t instead of the regular value function V_t is that it is very easy to compute the optimal action: you simply take the maximum of a number of Q-values. The disadvantage is the increase in required memory: you have to store a value of each (s,a)-couple. The main advantage however is its use in model-free techniques such as Q-learning, which is a method to approximate the Q-values.

Now we move to an online learning situation in which we want to estimate the Q-values while we control the system. Suppose the current state is s_t, we choose (for some reason) a_t, and we observe a reward r_t and a transition to s_{t+1} where we choose a_{t+1}. Then at first sight, a logical recursion for the approximate Q-values $\hat{Q}_t$ could be:

$$\hat{Q}_{t+1}(s_t, a_t) = r_t + \hat{Q}_t(s_{t+1}, a_{t+1}).$$

However, this shows quite some fluctuations. We need to smooth the values in a way similar to the smoothing method of Equation (4.1):

$$\hat{Q}_{t+1}(s_t, a_t) = \beta\left(r_t + \alpha\hat{Q}_t(s_{t+1}, a_{t+1})\right) + (1 - \beta)\hat{Q}_t(s_t, a_t).$$

This is called *Q-learning*, and β is called the *learning rate*.

We have not yet discussed how to choose the actions. Taking a_{t+1} equal to the maximizer of $\hat{Q}_t(s_{t+1}, a)$ is called *greedy*. It does not explore; it is a full exploitation policy. Taking a random action with a certain probability and greedy otherwise is called ϵ-greedy. Another solution for introducing exploration is starting with high initial values $\hat{Q}_0$. As a result, actions which have not been chosen often will still have a high value and will therefore be chosen. This is called *optimistic Q-learning*. We apply these ideas to the example studied earlier.

Example 9.7 *Consider again the problem of selecting the best of two treatments. As there are no states, there are only 2 Q-values to estimate, one for each treatment. The greedy policy has the possibility of not finding the best treatment, because when you start with a failure, that treatment will not be selected anymore. ϵ-greedy and optimistic learning will (likely) find the best treatment, but at the price of selecting the suboptimal treatment more often than necessary. The advantage is evidently the low computational complexity of the method which pays off when the problem becomes more complicated.*

Exercise 9.5 *Consider a problem as in the example with (unknown) success probabilities of 0.4 and 0.6. Take $\alpha = 0.9$ and $\beta = 0.25$. Implement the three methods mentioned in R and simulate them many times for 100 consecutive patients. How often do they find the best treatment? What are the discounted values, averaged over the simulation runs?*
This exercise requires programming experience.

Just as their full-information counterparts, RL problems can also be high-dimensional. In this case Q-learning also becomes computationally infeasible. Then the same approach as in ADP can be used, approximating the value function using ML. This approach—thus combining ML with RL—is known under the name *deep reinforcement learning*. Expectations for this approach are high: it could lead to "profound transformations in information and communication technologies, with applications in clinical decision support, marketing, finance, resource management, autonomous driving, robotics, smart grids, and more", according to [5].

Box 9.5. Games

Many games such as Connect Four, Chess and Go can also be formulated as DP problems, with the exception that they alternate minimization and maximization. However, methods based on backward recursion do not work very well: many of the states you end up analyzing will never occur or are simply impossible to occur. For this reason, a forward tree search, enumerating many possibilities starting from the initial state, is a better approach. For simple games such as Tic-tac-toe or Connect Four the full tree can be enumerated and therefore solved. For more difficult games such as Chess and Go this is impossible and heuristics are required. The most successful method is *Monte Carlo tree search* (MCTS). It builds up a tree with moves it already analyzed. From the last position, it randomly simulates the game until it finishes. With this outcome the starting leaf is updated as well as all branches of the tree above it. Now the next game to be simulated is selected by making moves in the tree in a bandit-like manner until a leaf is reached. From there a new leaf is constructed and analyzed, etc. This way the algorithm can build up a game tree by playing against itself. Finally the move is selected which has the highest proportion of games won in its subtree. A graphical illustration of MCTS is below (from [4]). This algorithm is the basis of the AlphaGo program that has beaten the Go world champion in 2017.

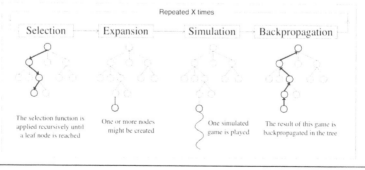

9.6   Additional reading

Puterman [31] and Kallenberg [19] are mathematically-oriented text books on the subject of this chapter. Sutton & Barto [39] is a text by the founders of reinforcement learning. Bertsekas & Tsitsiklis [2] made approximate DP popular. Powell [30] is a relatively recent text on the same subject.

Cross [6] is an entertaining non-technical text on revenue management. François-Lavet et al. [5] is a recent introduction to deep RL.

Chapter 10

Answers to Exercises

Below you can find answers to exercises and some R code. Documents with all R code and answers to Excel exercises can be downloaded from gerkoole.com/IBA.

Answer to Exercise 2.1
For somebody who is born on Jan 14, 1971, at 7:30, the answers could be:
```
> Sys.Date()-as.Date("1971-1-14")
> as.double(Sys.time())-as.double(strptime("1971-1-14 07:30",
    "%Y-%m-%d %H:%M"))
```

Answer to Exercise 2.2
A possible answer:
```
> fam = data.frame(names=c("G","L","P","E"),
    sex=c("m","m","m","f"),
    bd=c("1964-7-27","1990-2-10","1996-11-10","2002-1-27"))
> fam$bd=as.Date(fam$bd)
> fam$age=floor(as.integer(Sys.Date()-fam$bd)/365)
> tapply(fam$age,fam$sex,mean)
> fam$names[which.max(fam[fam$sex=="m",]$bd)]
```

Answer to Exercise 3.1
```
> library(datasets)
> mean(eurodist);mean(eurodist,trim=0.4);median(eurodist)
> sd(eurodist);var(eurodist)
> x=rep(1,100)
> mean(x);mean(x,trim=0.4);median(x);sd(x);var(x)
```

137

```
> x[20:30]=2
> mean(x);mean(x,trim=0.4);median(x);sd(x);var(x)
```

Answer to Exercise 3.2
```
> AP=AirPassengers
> quantile(AP,c(0,0.25,0.5,0.75,1))
> mean(AP);sd(AP)
> hist(AP)
> boxplot(AP)
```

Answer to Exercise 3.3
The possible outcomes are 0, 1, 2 and 3, with respective probabilities (approximately): $0.3, 0.8 - 0.3 = 0.5$, $0.95 - 0.8 = 0.15, 1 - 0.95 = 0.05$.

Answer to Exercise 3.4
```
> dbinom(0,10,1/6);(5/6)^10
> plot(0:10,dbinom(0:10,10,1/6))
```

Answer to Exercise 3.5

$$\mathbb{E}\overline{X} = \mathbb{E}\frac{X_1 + \cdots + X_n}{n} = \frac{\mathbb{E}(X_1 + \cdots + X_n)}{n} =$$

$$\frac{\mathbb{E}X_1 + \cdots + \mathbb{E}X_n}{n} = \frac{n\mathbb{E}X_1}{n} = \mathbb{E}X_1;$$

$$\sigma^2(\overline{X}) = \sigma^2\left(\frac{X_1 + \cdots + X_n}{n}\right) = \frac{\sigma^2(X_1 + \cdots + X_n)}{n^2} =$$

$$\frac{n\sigma^2(X_1)}{n^2} = \frac{\sigma^2(X_1)}{n}$$

and thus

$$\sigma(\overline{X}) = \frac{\sigma(X_1)}{\sqrt{n}}$$

Answer to Exercise 3.6
```
> sample=rbinom(1000,1,0.5)
> av=matrix()
> for(n in 1:1000)av[n]=mean(sample[1:n])
> plot(av,type="l")
```
This illustrates the LLN because for larger n we see that the average converges to 0.5 which is the expected value.

Answer to Exercise 3.7
a. mean((sample(6,10000,replace=T)+
    sample(6,10000,replace=T) == 10))
b. There are 3 combinations leading to 10: 4-6, 5-5, and 6-4. Thus the probability of 10 equals $3/36 = 0.0833$.

Answer to Exercise 3.8

$$\lim_{n\to\infty} \mathbb{P}(N_n = k) = \lim_{n\to\infty} \binom{n}{k}\left(\frac{\lambda}{n}\right)^k\left(1 - \frac{\lambda}{n}\right)^{n-k} =$$

$$\frac{\lambda^k}{k!} \lim_{n\to\infty}\left(1 - \frac{\lambda}{n}\right)^n \frac{n!}{(n-k)!(n-\lambda)^k} = \frac{\lambda^k}{k!}e^{-\lambda},$$

which is the Poisson distribution. The crucial step in the last equality is to see that $(1 - \lambda/n)^n \to e^{-\lambda}$. See the Wikipedia page "list of limits", it is the first "notable special limit" with $k = -\lambda$ and $m = 1$.

Answer to Exercise 3.9
a. The answer of sd(rpois(1000,10)) is close to $\sqrt{10}$ which is the square root of the variance, as expected.
b. > plot(0:30,dpois(0:30,1))
> lines(0:30,dpois(0:30,5),type="p",col="red")
> lines(0:30,dpois(0:30,20),type="p",col="green")

Answer to Exercise 3.10
mean(pmax(rpois(10000,90)-100,0))/90 or
    sum(dpois(101:200,90)*(1:100))/90.

Answer to Exercise 3.11
1/4, because the interval [0.5,1] is a quarter of the interval [0,2]. In R:
> s=runif(10000,0,2); mean(s>0.5&s<1)
and > punif(1,0,2)-punif(0.5,0,2)

Answer to Exercise 3.12
> pnorm(0)
> 1-pnorm(1); pnorm(1)-pnorm(0)
> qnorm(0.95)

Answer to Exercise 3.13
a. 1-pnorm(0,2,10); mean(rnorm(100000,2,10)>0)
b. multiply by σ and add μ.

Answer to Exercise 3.14
```
> hist(rnorm(10000)+rnorm(10000));
> hist(rnorm(10000)-rnorm(10000)) is also normal because −Y is;
> hist(runif(10000)+runif(10000)) is neither uniform nor normal but
```
triangular.

Answer to Exercise 3.15
```
pnorm(1)-pnorm(-1); pnorm(2)-pnorm(-2)
```

Answer to Exercise 3.16
The expected length of a block of 8 operations is $8 * 40 = 400$ minutes, the
SD is $\sqrt{8 * 20^2} = 56.6$ minutes. The probability of being late is

$$1 - \text{pnorm}(7 * 60, 400, 56.6)$$

which is around 36%.

From the formulas of the expectation and SD of the uniform distribution
it follows that $a + b = 100$ and $(b - a)/\sqrt{12} = 20$. Some computations show
that $a = 50 - 10\sqrt{12} = 15.4$ and $b = 50 + 10\sqrt{12} = 84.6$. Then

$$\text{mean}(\text{rowSums}(\text{matrix}(\text{runif}(80000, a, b), \text{ncol} = 8)) > 7 * 60)$$

is again close to 36%.

Answer to Exercise 3.17
When looking at the cdf in Figure 3.8, an x-value of around 20 corresponds
to a y-value of 0.5. This is confirmed by computations: `qlnorm(0.5,3,0.5)`
and `exp(qnorm(0.5,3,0.5))` give both 20.09.

Answer to Exercise 3.18
Again lognormal. The reason is as follows: Let X and Y be normal and thus
e^X and e^Y are lognormal. Then the product $e^X e^Y = e^{X+Y}$ is again lognormal
because $X + Y$ is normal.

Answer to Exercise 3.19
```
> mu=log(10^2/(sqrt(5^2+10^2))); sd=sqrt(log(1+5^2/10^2))
> mean(rlnorm(10000,mu,sd)); sd(rlnorm(10000,mu,sd))
```

Answer to Exercise 3.20

$$\mathbb{E} \sum_{i=1}^{n} (X_i - \overline{X})^2 = \sum_{i=1}^{n} \mathbb{E}(X_i - \overline{X})^2 = n\mathbb{E}(X_1 - \overline{X})^2 =$$

$$\frac{1}{n}\mathbb{E}((n-1)X_1 - (X_2 + \cdots + X_n))^2.$$

Working out the multiplication leads to terms of the form $\mathbb{E}X_i^2 = \mathbb{E}X_1^2$ and $\mathbb{E}X_i X_j = (\mathbb{E}X_1)^2$. Many of the terms cancel out; what remains is $(n-1)(\mathbb{E}X_1^2 - (\mathbb{E}X_1)^2)$. From this it follows that $(\mathbb{E}S)^2 = \sigma^2$.

Answer to Exercise 3.21
```
c(9.8-qt(0.95,199)*5.4/sqrt(199),
    9.8+qt(0.95,199)*5.4/sqrt(199)).
```

Answer to Exercise 3.22
a. The answer is 2. If you roll a die once the expected number of 6s is $1/6$, thus 12 rolls gives expectation 2. You can also simulate it with:
```
> mean(rbinom(10000,12,1/6))
```
b. The command `binom.test(0,12,1/6)` gives as p-value 0.24, thus the null-hypothesis that the die is unbiased is not rejected.

Answer to Exercise 3.23
The answer is 1.8×10^{-46}, thus significantly different. Thus can be obtained in the following ways:
```
> t.test(beaver1$temp,mu=37.3)
> 2*pt(sqrt(length(beaver1$temp))*(mean(beaver1$temp)-37.3)/
    sd(beaver1$temp),length(beaver1$temp)-1)
```

Answer to Exercise 3.24
```
> t=(mean(beaver1$temp)-mean(beaver2$temp))/
    sqrt(var(beaver1$temp)/length(beaver1$temp)
    +var(beaver2$temp)/length(beaver2$temp))
```
Because `pnorm(t)` is very small the null hypothesis is rejected. This result can also be obtained by executing `t.test(beaver1$temp,beaver2$temp)`.

Answer to Exercise 3.25
a. We use the command `hist(Nile)`, `boxplot(Nile)` and `qqnorm(Nile)`. The Q-Q plot is close to straight but not quite therefore it won't be normal.
b. The finding under a is confirmed by `shapiro.test(Nile)`.

c. The CI can obtained by
```
> c(mean(Nile)-1.96*sd(Nile)/sqrt(length(Nile)),
    mean(Nile)+1.96*sd(Nile)/sqrt(length(Nile))).
```
d. `t.test(Nile[1:50],Nile[51:100])` gives a p-value close to 10^{-4}, thus there is evidence of a difference.

Answer to Exercise 4.1
```
> library(datasets)
> m=mean(na.omit(airquality$Solar.R))
> airquality$Solar.R[is.na(airquality$Solar.R)]=m
```

Answer to Exercise 4.2
```
> centers=kmeans(rock,3)$centers
> plot(rock[,1:2])
> points(centers[,1:2],pch=3,cex=1.5)
```
A choice of 2 centers would have been better.

Answer to Exercise 4.3
```
> attach(longley)
> finalmodel=lm(Employed~GNP+Unemployed)
> newdata=data.frame(GNP.deflator=mean(GNP.deflator),
    GNP=mean(GNP),Unemployed=mean(Unemployed),
    Armed.Forces=mean(Armed.Forces),Population=mean(Population),
    Year=mean(Year))
> predict(finalmodel,newdata)
```
with value 65.317.

Answer to Exercise 4.4
```
summary(lm(y~poly(x,2),data=df))
```

Answer to Exercise 4.5
All interactions can be added by `Ozone~(.)^2`. However, applying step down now becomes a tedious job. A significant model with a higher R^2 is: `Ozone~Wind*Temp+Month`.

Answer to Exercise 4.6
```
summary(lm(len~supp+factor(dose),data=ToothGrowth))
```
; OJ and 2.

Answer to Exercise 4.7

```
> 1-sum((aq$Ozone-fit)^2)/sum((aq$Ozone-mean(aq$Ozone))^2)
```

gives an R squared of around 0.85 while the linear model of Exercise 4.5 gave an R squared of 0.64.

Using

```
> train_set = sample(nrow(aq),round(0.7*nrow(aq)))
> train = aq[train_set,]
> test = aq[-train_set,]
```

a training and a test set can be constructed. Now the linear model and the neural can be trained as before and the R squared calculated for both. They fluctuate a lot because of the small sample size, most of the time lower than the in-sample value and closer to each other. Note that R squared can even be negative in the case of a really bad predictor. In fact, for test sets it is more common to use the RMSE.

Answer to Exercise 4.8

The answer is around 6. Scaling is required, and because the `neuralnets` library cannot handle categorical attributes you have to transform the attribute `species` with 3 possible values to 2 dummy variables. See the R code on `gerkoole.com/IBA` for more details.

Answer to Exercise 4.9

Using `rpart(Ozone~.,data=aq)` the decision tree can be constructed. The R squared is 0.70.

With a training and a test set the R squared is lower but varies, depending on the random selection of the test set.

Answer to Exercise 4.10

Similar to the previous question, the R command is `randomForest`. The in sample R squared is 0.91.

Answer to Exercise 4.11

The following R code does the trick:

```
> library(xgboost)
> aq=na.omit(airquality)
> data=data.matrix(aq[,-1]); labels=data.matrix(aq[,1])
> boosted_tree = xgboost(data,label=labels,nrounds=10)
> pred = predict(boosted_tree,data)
> 1-sum((labels-pred)^2)/sum((labels-mean(labels))^2)
```

The construction of the training and test set can be done in the usual way. Note that
```
> xgb.cv(data=data,label=labels,nfold=5,nrounds=10)
```
can be used for cross-validation.

Answer to Exercise 4.12
The answers are: 5.64, 5.39 and 5.39 (with `nrounds=10`). Unfortunately the data formats of the libraries are slightly different, requiring some pre-processing.

Answer to Exercise 4.13
The forecast with the log scale is slightly better, the RMSEs are 47.9 and 46.9. The log scale captures the amplitude better, but it overestimates the trend.

Answer to Exercise 4.14
```
> fc=forecast(hw(window(AirPassengers,end=c(1958,12))))$mean
> sqrt(mean((fc-AirPassengers[121:144])^2))
```
give as RMSE 46.9.

Answer to Exercise 4.15
Some R commands with a test set of 4 years:
```
> fc_hw = hw(window(UKgas,end=c(1982,4)),h=16)
> sqrt(mean((fc_hw$mean-window(UKgas,start=c(1983,1)))^2))
> fc_arima = forecast(auto.arima(window(UKgas,end=c(1982,4))),
        h=16)
```
The RMSE of HW is 49.3, of ARIMA 40.7. The result for HW can be improved slightly by tuning the parameters. Note that the `hw` R function already determines optimal parameters based on repeated training and testing. As a result the possible improvements are very limited.

Answer to Exercise 4.16
$156/(156+112) = 58\%$, $445/(55+445) = 89\%$, and $156/(156+55) = 74\%$. The plot with sensitivity and specificity (dashed) should be as below. The full code can be found online.

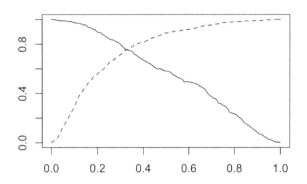

Answer to Exercise 4.17

0.15, with 12 FN and 270 FP, with costs 390 times the costs of a FP.

Answer to Exercise 4.18

For our choice of training and test set the confusion matrices are very similar:

```
              actuals                        actuals
predictions pos neg        predictions pos neg
        pos  52  26                pos  51   25
        neg  28 124                neg  29  125
```

For this reason the choice of method will not depend on the outcomes, but on the algorithm. Because of its simplicity and interpretability, logistic regression is preferred. Note that the ANN might be better tuned, potentially leading to better results. The full code can be found online.

Answer to Exercise 4.19

Using `rpart` on the training and `predict` on the test set leads to the confusion matrix below. The code can be found online.

```
                  actuals
predictions pos neg
        pos  53   30
        neg  27  120
```

Answer to Exercise 4.20

Using `svm` on the training and `predict` on the test set leads to the confusion matrix below, which is slightly different. The code can be found online.

```
                          actuals
              predictions pos neg
                      pos  47  19
                      neg  33 131
```

Answer to Exercise 5.1
a. `max` computes the maximum over all its arguments, thus the output is a single number. `pmax` takes several vectors and gives as output the component-wise maximum, thus a vector.
b. A 95% CI using 10000 simulations is $[8.15, 8.19]$. Answers differ depending on the samples. The code can be found online.
c. A 95% CI using 10000 simulations is $[8.57, 8.65]$.

Answer to Exercise 5.2
See the online Excel file.

Answer to Exercise 5.3
a. In most cases you will get a CI which includes 100000, the width depends on the number of simulations.
b. The expectation is 100000 by properties of the normal distribution, no simulation needed.
c. Around $[0.32, 0.34]$ for 10000 simulations. Note that there is no easy formula to obtain this number, we either need simulation or advanced mathematics.

Answer to Exercise 5.4
The expected number of transferred patients is around 1.8, the width of the CI depending on the number of simulation runs. The code can be found online.

Answer to Exercise 6.1
The R code is
```
> library(lpSolve)
> con=matrix(c(1,3,2,1,0,3),nrow=2,byrow=TRUE)
> lp("max",c(2,4,8),con,c("<=","<="),c(10,12))$solution
```
with solution $(0, 0.66, 4)$ and value 34.66.

Answer to Exercise 6.2
a. The R code is
```
> con=matrix(c(1,-2,2,-1,-1,3,1,-1,1),nrow=3,byrow=TRUE)
```

```
> lp("min",c(2,1,4),con,c("<=","=",">="),c(120,100,80))
```
with solution $(40, 10, 50)$ and value 290.

b. Max $-2x_1 - x_2 - 4x_3$ subject to $x_1 - 2x_2 + 2x_3 \leq 120$, $-x_1 - x_2 + 3x_3 \leq 100$, $x_1 + x_2 - 3x_3 \leq -100$, $-x_1 + x_2 - x_3 \leq -80$, and all $x_i \geq 0$.

c. The R code is

```
> con=matrix(c(1,-2,2,-1,-1,3,1,1,-3,-1,1,-1),nrow=4,
    byrow=TRUE)
> lp("max",c(-2,-1,-4),con,rep("<=",4),c(120,100,-100,-80)).
```

Answer to Exercise 6.3

The R code is:

```
> lp("max",c(1,1),matrix(c(1,1,-1,-1),nrow=2),c(">","<"),
    c(-1,1))
> lp("max",c(0,1),matrix(c(1,1,1,0),nrow=2),c("<",">"),
    c(1,2))
```

Answer to Exercise 6.4

See the online Excel file.

Answer to Exercise 6.5

See the online Excel file.

Answer to Exercise 6.6

See the online Excel file.

Answer to Exercise 6.7

The shortest finish time is 8. For the model, see the online Excel file.

Answer to Exercise 6.8

The optimal objective value is 38. For the model, see the online Excel file.

Answer to Exercise 6.9

See the online Excel file.

Answer to Exercise 6.10

In R:

```
> lp("max",c(60,60,40,10,20,10,3),matrix(c(3,5,4,1.3,3,3,1),
    nrow=1,byrow=TRUE),"<=",11,all.bin=TRUE)$solution
```
See online for the Excel file.

Answer to Exercise 6.11

The items are ordered in decreasing reward per unit of volume. Thus it is optimal to take the low-numbered items as much as possible, unless prohibited by the branching variables set to 0. This leads to the following branch-and bound tree:

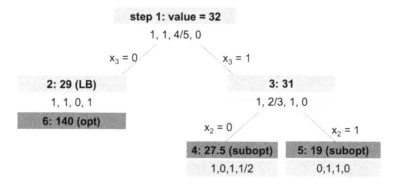

The R code is:

```
> lp("max",c(15,9,10,5),matrix(c(1,3,5,4),nrow=1,byrow=TRUE),
    "<=",8,all.bin=TRUE)$solution
```

Answer to Exercise 6.12

The minimal value is 14. For the model, see the online Excel file.

Answer to Exercise 6.13

See the online Excel file.

Answer to Exercise 6.14

See the online Excel file.

Answer to Exercise 6.15

See the online Excel file

Answer to Exercise 6.16

See the online Excel file.

Answer to Exercise 6.18

The optimal objective value is 77, using 5 links. For the model, see the online Excel file.

Answer to Exercise 6.19

The problem now becomes:

$$\text{minimize} \sum_{t=1}^{T}(c_t x_t + h_t s_t + K y_t)$$

subject to

$s_{t+1} = s_t - d_{t+1} + x_{t+1}$ for $t = 1, \ldots, T-1$;

$x_t \leq M y_t$ for $t = 1, \ldots, T$;

$x_t, s_t \geq 0, y_t \in \{0, 1\}$ for $t = 1, \ldots, T$;

$M \gg 0$.

Answer to Exercise 6.20

See the online Excel file.

Answer to Exercise 6.21

See the online AMPL files.

Answer to Exercise 6.22

See the online Excel file.

Answer to Exercise 7.1

Using Dijkstra's algorithm gives:

	distances				
step	A	B	C	D	E
1	0	∞	∞	∞	∞
2		10	2	21	∞
3		5		3	13
4				10	13
5					12

The LO formulation is as follows:

$$\text{minimize } 10x_{AB} + 2x_{AC} + 21x_{AD} + 5x_{BD} + 3x_{CB} + 11x_{CE} + 2x_{DE}$$

subject to

$x_{AB} + x_{AC} + x_{AD} = 1$;

$x_{AB} + x_{CB} = x_{BD}; x_{AC} = x_{CB} + x_{CE}; x_{AD} + X_{BD} = x_{DE};$

$x_{ij} \geq 0$.

The optimal solution is $x_{AC} = x_{CB} = x_{BD} = x_{DE} = 1, x_{AB} = x_{AD} = x_{CE} = 0$. All constraints are satisfied for this solution.

Answer to Exercise 7.2

See the online AMPL files.

Answer to Exercise 7.3
A possible series of augmenting paths is as follows:
- ABDFH with value 2;
- ACEGH with value 1;
- ACBGEH with value 2;
- ACDEH with value 1.
No more augmenting path can be found, you cannot reach {E,F,G,H} any-more. Thus the max flow is 6, and this is indeed the value of the cut between {A,B,C,D} and {E,F,G,H}.
    See online for the AMPL file with the LO code.

Answer to Exercise 7.4
Taking out BD and CE, thereby constructing the tour ABEFDCA leads to a reduction in length of 1. No further improvements are possible.

Answer to Exercise 7.5
Using the TSP R package the same tour is in Exercise 7.4 is found. See the online file for the code.

Answer to Exercise 8.1
a. We cannot tell which one is better because the CI contains 0 most of the times. If we increase the number of simulations to 1M we see that the first product is better.
b. This question can be answered using the property of normal distributions on page 44. The CI is narrower, but still contains 0 most of the time.

Answer to Exercise 8.2
a. The optimal order quantity π is 12 and its value ± 2.56.
b. The optimal π and its value change and are often > 2.56.
The code can be found online.

Answer to Exercise 8.3
The algorithm finds the optimal solution 12 most of the time. The code can be found online.

Answer to Exercise 8.4
The algorithm finds again the optimal solution 12 most of the time. The code can be found online. For a typical run of the algorithm the following solutions are found as the algorithm progresses:

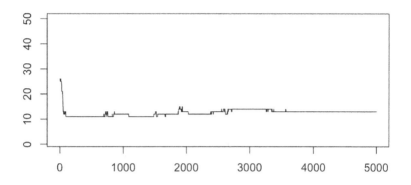

Answer to Exercise 9.1

As an example, we compute $V_3(C)$. It is given by:

$$V_3(C) = \min\{1 + V_2(A), 1 + V_2(B), 2 + V_2(D), 4 + V_2(E)\} =$$

$$\min\{\infty, 9, 5, 6\} = 5$$

with minimizing action D.

Answer to Exercise 9.2

Using DP gives:

step	distances				
	A	B	C	D	E
0	∞	∞	∞	∞	0
1	∞	∞	11	2	0
2	13	7	11	2	0
3	13	7	9	2	0
4	12	7	9	2	0

Answer to Exercise 9.3

The last weeks the decrease for high-prices rooms increases, making it advantageous to sell only high-priced rooms. Earlier in time this is not the case, therefore when there is enough capacity the low price is offered. As the remaining demand decreases over time, you offer the low price with less remaining capacity.

b. See the online file. The total expected revenue is € 5341.5.

c. See the R file with answers.

Answer to Exercise 9.4

See the separate R file.

Answer to Exercise 9.5
See the separate R file.

Bibliography

[1] INFORMS Analytics Maturity Model. Available online at `https://analyticsmaturity.informs.org`.

[2] D.P. Bertsekas and J.N. Tsitsiklis. *Neuro-Dynamic Programming*. Athena Scientific, 1996.

[3] J. Bisschop. *AIMMS Optimization Modeling*. AIMMS, Haarlem, 2016. Downloadable from AIMMS website.

[4] G. Chaslot, M. Winands, van den Herik, H., J. Uiterwijk, and B. Bouzy. Progressive strategies for Monte-Carlo tree search. *New Mathematics and Natural Computation*, 4:343–357, 2008.

[5] V. François-Lavet, P. Henderson, R. Islam, M.G. Bellemare, and J. Pineau. An introduction to deep reinforcement learning. *Foundations and Trends in Machine Learning*, 11(3–4), 2018.

[6] R.G. Cross. *Revenue Management: Hard-Core Tactics for Market Domination*. Broadway Books, 1998.

[7] G.B. Dantzig. A comment on Edie's "Traffic delays at toll booths". *Journal of the Operations Research Society of America*, 2(3):339–341, 1954.

[8] T.H. Davenport and J.G. Harris. *Competing on Analytics: The New Science of Winning*. Harvard Business School, 2007.

[9] J.W. Foreman. *Data Smart*. Wiley, 2013.

[10] R. Fourer, D.M. Gay, and B.W. Kernighan. *AMPL: A Modeling Language for Mathematical Programming*. Duxbury, Thomson, 2003. Available online at `http://ampl.com/resources/the-ampl-book`.

[11] M.C. Fu. Optimization for simulation: Theory vs. practice. *INFORMS Journal on Computing*, 14:192–215, 2002.

[12] A. Géron. *Hands-On Machine Learning with Scikit-Learn and TensorFlow*. O'Reilly, 2017.

[13] B. Guenin, J. Könemann, and L. Tunçel. *A Gentle Introduction to Optimization*. Cambridge University Press, 2014.

[14] C.M. Harris, S.P. Murphy, and M. Vaisman. *Analyzing the Analyzers*. O'Reilly Media, 2013.

[15] P. E. Hart, N.J. Nilsson, and B. Raphael. A formal basis for the heuristic determination of minimum cost paths. *IEEE Transactions on Systems Science and Cybernetics*, SSC-4(2):100–107, 1968.

[16] T. Hastie, R. Tibshirani, and J. Friedman. *The Elements of Statistical Learning*. Springer, 2nd edition, 2017.

[17] F.S. Hillier and G.J. Lieberman. *Introduction to Operations Research*. McGraw-Hill, 8th edition, 2005.

[18] R.J. Hyndman and G. Athanasopoulos. *Forecasting: Principles and Practice*. O Texts, 2018.

[19] L.C.M. Kallenberg. Markov Decision Processes. Unpublished textbook. Downloadable from `http://goo.gl/5nnKN7`, 2018.

[20] W.D. Kelton, R.P. Sandowski, and D.A. Sandowski. *Simulation with Arena*. McGraw-Hill, 1998.

[21] T. Klastorin. *Project Management: Techniques and Tradeoffs*. Wiley, 2003.

[22] J.P. Kotter. *Leading Change*. Harvard Business School Press, 1996.

[23] M. Kuhn and K. Johnson. *Applied Predictive Modeling*. Springer, 2013.

[24] S. Makridakis, E. Spiliotis, and V. Assimakopoulos. The M4 competition: Results, findings, conclusion and way forward. *International Journal of Forecasting*, 34:802–808, 2018.

[25] C.D. Manning, P. Raghavan, and H. Schutze. *Introduction to Information Retrieval*. Cambridge University Press, 2008.

[26] B.L. Nelson. *Foundations and Methods of Stochastic Simulation*. Springer, 2013.

[27] K. O'Neil. *Weapons of Math Destruction*. Crown Books, 2016.

[28] C.H. Papadimitriou and K. Steiglitz. *Combinatorial Optimization: Algorithms and Complexity*. Dover, 1998.

[29] S.G. Powell, K.R. Baker, and B. Lawson. Impact of errors in operational spreadsheets. *Decision Support Systems*, 7:126–132, 2009.

[30] W.B. Powell. *Approximate Dynamic Programming: Solving the Curses of Dimensionality*. Wiley, 2nd edition, 2011.

[31] M.L. Puterman. *Markov Decision Processes*. Wiley, 1994.

[32] R.L. Rardin. *Optimization in Operations Research*. Pearson, 2014.

[33] S.M. Ross. *Simulation*. Academic Press, 6th edition, 1996.

[34] S.M. Ross. *A First Course in Probability*. Prentice Hall, 6th edition, 2002.

[35] S. Sashihara. *The Optimization Edge*. McGraw Hill, 2011.

[36] S. Savage. *The Flaw of Averages: Why We Underestimate Risk in the Face of Uncertainty*. Wiley, 2012.

[37] D. Schultes. *Route Planning in Road Networks*. PhD thesis, Universität Fridericiana zu Karlsruhe, 2008.

[38] J. Silge and D. Robinson. *Text Mining with R*. O'Reilly, 2018.

[39] R.S. Sutton and A.G. Barto. *Reinforcement Learning: An Introduction*. MIT Press, 2000.

[40] H.A. Taha. *Operation Research: An Introduction*. Prentice Hall, 6th edition, 1997.

[41] M.F. Triola. *Elementary Statistics*. Pearson, 13th edition, 2017.

[42] W.L. Winston. *Operations Research: Applications and Algorithms*. Duxbury Press, 1987.

Index